# Classic Cars

## Celebrating The Legends

Tim Slade

**igloo**

# igloo

Published in 2006
by Igloo Books Ltd
Cottage Farm,
Sywell,
NN6 0JB.
www.igloo-books.com

ISBN 1-84561-430-5

Project management by: Metro Media Ltd
Editorial and design management: Cecilia Thom
Author: Tim Slade
Sub-Editors: Cyrus Shahrad, Cecilia Thom
Layout: Richard Reid, Z Swaleh, Cecilia Thom
Cover: Joel Rojas, Cecilia Thom
Cover pictures contributed by: National Motor Museum/MPL, Tim Slade
Pictures contributed by: ActionLibrary.com, LAT Photographic,
National Motor Museum/MPL, SeriousWheels.com, Tim Slade

Printed in China

# Contents

| | | | |
|---|---|---|---|
| Introduction | 4 | 1959 Jaguar Mk II | 86 |
| 1901 Curved Dash Oldsmobile | 12 | 1959 Austin-Healey Sprite | 90 |
| 1908 Model T Ford | 14 | 1959 Cadillac | 92 |
| 1922 Austin Seven | 18 | 1959 Mini | 96 |
| 1924 Bentley 3.0 ltr | 22 | 1960 Ferrari 250GT SWB | 100 |
| 1926 Bugatti Type 35/35B | 26 | 1960 Mercedes Benz 180 | 104 |
| 1928 Duesenberg Model J | 30 | 1961 Jaguar E-type | 106 |
| 1932 '32 Ford | 34 | 1962 MGB | 110 |
| 1934 Mercedes 500K/540K | 36 | 1962 Ford Cortina | 114 |
| 1935 Auburn 851/852 Speedster | 40 | 1962 AC Cobra | 118 |
| 1936 Rolls-Royce Phantom III | 44 | 1963 Studebaker Avanti | 122 |
| 1936 Cord 810/812 | 46 | 1963 Chevrolet Corvette Stingray | 126 |
| 1941 Jeep | 50 | 1964 Ford Mustang | 130 |
| 1946 MG TC | 54 | 1964 Pontiac GTO | 134 |
| 1946 VW Beetle | 58 | 1964 Porsche 911 | 136 |
| 1951 Hudson Hornet | 62 | 1966 Alfa Romeo Duetto | 140 |
| 1954 Mercedes 300SL | 64 | 1966 Lamborghini Miura | 144 |
| 1955 Citroen DS | 68 | 1966 Dodge Charger | 148 |
| 1955 '55-'57 Ford Thunderbird | 72 | 1968 Scimitar GTE | 152 |
| 1955 '55, '56, '57 Chevrolets | 76 | 1969 Datsun 240Z | 154 |
| 1958 Aston Martin DB4/DB5 | 80 | 1973 BMW 3.0 CSL | 156 |
| 1959 Facel Vega HK500 | 84 | | |

What is it that attracts people to classic cars? Why bother spending so much time and money on old motor cars when you could have a perfectly good modern one, and enjoy clean fingernails and a healthy bank balance? Perhaps we need to start with the question – what exactly is a classic car? The obvious answer that most of us would come up with, is that a classic car is an old car. In fact the word 'classic' seems to have been commandeered just lately and redefined as an alternative for old. Of course the term 'classic' means far more than simply aged. It implies that something is, 'of the first rank or authority'. Plainly there is a lot more to this classic car thing than simply age. Does dodging the crusher for a few years really turn any car into a classic? Well, it's going to upset a few

old car owners, but there is a bit more to it than that.

The cars that we've chosen for this book are pretty much all models that you are going to find it tough to argue against. It was no easy task to whittle down the tens of thousands of models built since Karl Benz took his three-wheeler onto the streets of Mannheim in 1885. There are many different ways to earn the moniker 'classic', and for every car here, there is a different combination of these reasons.

Breaking new ground is perhaps the most sure-fire way to earn your 'classic' status. The Mini, the Model T, the Beetle, the Citroen DS and even the Reliant Scimitar GTE can claim their place on this count. Providing reliable and much loved transport for

vast numbers of people is another reason, claimed by the Model T and the Ford Cortina among others. Success in competition is an excellent reason, and here the Mini and the Cortina start racking up the points, along with the Porsche 911 and the Ferrari 250 SWB. Domination of NASCAR means that the Hudson Hornet has no trouble getting through the door of the classics club.

Then there is the little matter of desire. There are cars that inspire the sin of covetousness in just about anyone who lays eyes on them. How do you avoid wanting a Mercedes 300SL or an Aston Martin DB4? Although, perhaps it was the designers of the '30s who best knew how to tap into those parts of our brain that make us want and desire; the Duesenberg S and Mercedes

'K' cars appear to have been styled with little other than automotive lust in mind. The Mercedes 540K Special Roadster did such a good job that even so many decades later it still has much to do with our perception of the Mercedes brand.

So what are the factors that fail to convey classic status? Performance alone is not enough, and there have been some ugly Ferraris and Lamborghinis that are beaten to the classic finishing line by the humble Fiat 500. Huge production figures won't necessarily get you there either. Many cars sold well but failed entirely to generate affection in their owners. Generally these models have simply vanished, as no one felt motivated to make the effort necessary to keep them going. When did you last see an Austin Maxi or a Hillman Avenger? Even expensive cars went this way. What happened to all the Jaguar Mk Xs and Humber Super Snipes?

With cars having been around since 1885 it makes for an intriguing question to ask when the concept of the classic car might have first appeared. Even the most avid classic car buff would have to admit that it has much to do with the preconception that, 'things ain't what they used to be'. So, when did people start to yearn for the charms of earlier times?

The old car enthusiast may have been around rather longer than expected. In the early years, automobile advances came thick and fast, making cars obsolete often before they were even

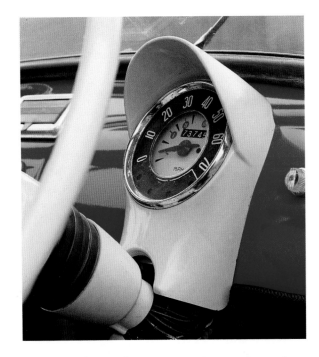

delivered. And yet, at a time when the excitement and romance of the motor car was all about the new, there is evidence that some motorists were already becoming attached to the old.

In October 1910 an article appeared in the British magazine *The Motor*, concerning a journey made in the car belonging to a friend of the author. The author claimed to have owned five different motor cars by this date, but his friend stuck with his first; a Benz from 1901. Even in 1910 this vehicle was considered an archaic contraption, and yet its owner professed many excellent reasons for preferring it to a more modern motor car. The solid tyres almost never wore out and, of course, there were no punctures to deal with. Another is that it travelled for 24 hilly miles on five pints of petrol – that's 38.4 miles to the gallon! Parsimony might have been his main reason for keeping his Benz, but a real affection for this antiquated automobile also shines through.

We have to wait until a few years later for the formalization of the 'things ain't what they used to be' ethos. It can be claimed with some authority that this came about in 1934, with the formation of the Vintage Sports Car Club, or VSCC. A group of enthusiasts met in a pub called the Phoenix at Harley Wintney, a village about thirty miles west of London. They were there to discuss a proposition – in a now long-defunct magazine called *The Light Car* – that a club should be formed for the 'not so rich'. They were concerned that the heyday of historic motoring was coming to an end, and they felt that mass production was leading to quantity being considered more important than quality – arguments that are hard to quarrel with. And so they formed a club to encourage the use of cars built before 31 December 1930. Things were not all bad, and an approved list of modern cars was drawn up. The VSCC now welcomes cars from this list built up until 1941, as well as anything made before 1931.

*The Humber Super Snipe may be an old car, but is it a classic car?*

The VSCC has endured and prospered, promoting racing and events for its members' cars, with fiercely fought racing, hill climbing and, improbably, trials over car-breaking dirt tracks. Members will even get their cars out for the New Year's Day lunchtime gathering at the Phoenix, where you will see vintage Lagondas and Bentleys, whatever the weather and however much salt there is on the roads.

Speaking of 'vintage', it might be best to clarify the meaning of the word. All vintage cars are welcome to the VSCC fold; ie those made before 31 December 1930. Many people believe any car made before the Second World War to be vintage; in fact the correct, though rather pedantic term, for cars made between 1931 and the war is, 'post vintage thoroughbred', or PVT. Quite where this leaves the less than thoroughbred is difficult to say.

The very earliest motor cars are referred to as 'veteran'. All the cars built before December 1904 are veterans. These are the cars that are eligible for the UK's famous London to Brighton run. Cars built between 1905 and 1918 are properly called 'Edwardians'.

There are many and varied reasons to endure the rigours that are an unavoidable part of classic car ownership. The essential one is using the car. You could say that if a car isn't driven then it becomes something else – a work of art, a museum piece,

a curio, a piece of junk, a waste of space or, perhaps, just forgotten. The essence of any motor car is in the driving – luckily this is a major motivation for most owners. A trip to the supermarket becomes a special event, and a sunny day is enough to provide an excuse for a drive. In London, for example, despite the traffic and terrible driving, it won't take long on a summer weekend before you see something special. It might be a Ferrari or a Morris 1000, but the enjoyment of using a classic is the same.

If you use your old car then it's very probable that you will want to use it for old-car events. If you are lucky enough to have a veteran, then the one event that can't be missed is the London to Brighton run. It is so popular that it can mean that a car made in 1904 will be worth many times the value of a similar 1905 car.

Held early in November every year, often in typically miserable English autumnal weather, there is always a good selection of registration plates from as far afield as the US and Australia. The number of cars taking part is something like a quite incredible 500. Some get little further than the gates of Hyde Park, London, where the run begins, but most make it to the seafront of Brighton. The event was first held in 1896 to celebrate that it had at last become legal for motor cars to be run upon English roads. The uniform 12mph speed limit would not have been a major inconvenience at the time. Held ever since, with breaks only for the two world wars, it's no surprise that it is the oldest consecutively held motoring event in the world.

The oldest competitive event, the Brighton Speed Trials, is held along the same stretch of road as the veteran's destination: Madeira Drive on Brighton seafront. It was first held in 1905, though due to disputes over the cost of resurfacing with the 'modern' tarmac it didn't happen again until 1923. Since 1932 it has only taken a break for the Second World War, and is still held every September. It is a fabulous place to see classics of all eras, on both two and four wheels, being given a real pasting.

It seems strange that anyone would want to risk their valuable, often temperamental and, quite possibly, irreplaceable classic by belting it around a race track. And yet all over the world there is historic racing taking place just about every summer weekend. In the US there are the legendary Monterey Historic

Automobile Races at the Laguna Seca circuit in California. These events have grown in stature every year since the races were first held in 1974 – it is unlikely that better classic racing will be seen anywhere in the US.

Part of the same weekend is the Pebble Beach concours, where the finest and most fabulous classic cars compete for the honour of being the best and most beautiful in the world. These are not cars that you will see on the street, no matter how perfect the weather.

In the UK it is the two events held at Goodwood that have captured everyone's imagination. The Festival of Speed is a hill climb held on roads through the glorious Goodwood estate in Sussex. A hill climb, or indeed a sprint, is an event where each car runs individually against the clock. First held in 1993 it instantly became a 'classic' in the old-car calendar. The combination of the country house location and the best competition cars from around the world being put through their paces is unmissable.

Later in the summer the Goodwood Revival meeting takes place, held at the historic Goodwood circuit nearby. The first event was only held in 1998, and yet it has come to be generally regarded as the finest historic automotive event in the world. Racing is for pre-1966 cars – the year that contemporary racing stopped at Goodwood. There are races for formula racing cars, sports cars and sports racing cars, as well as saloon cars. The attention to the pre-'66 detail is terrific, and it has become the biggest fancy dress party in the world, as most race-goers arrive in period costume. Many also arrive with period transport – the special pre-'66 visitors' car park is one of the largest classic car meetings all on its own.

Of course there are shows and gatherings for classics all over the world and to suit all tastes. Everything from one-marque meetings to enormous shows where 1,000 cars might turn up, to a few old cars brought together for the village fête.

One feature connects all these events: whether you drive a Rolls Royce or an Aston Martin, a Beetle or a Cortina, the enthusiasm is the same. It's the love for old cars that's important, and not the cost of your ride. The classic car world is anything but exclusive. At any event you go to you're going to find a bunch of friendly people who, given half a chance, will chat to you for the whole afternoon. Whether you own a classic car, or simply enjoy them, membership of one of the biggest, friendliest clubs in the world comes as part of the deal.

*Like a phoenix from the flames, the Curved Dash Olds became the first mass-produced car*

Ransom Eli Olds had been building experimental motor cars since 1887. By the 1890s, Olds had moved on to making gasoline-powered engines for use in factories and boats. It was in 1897 that he got serious about building motor cars, establishing the Olds Motor Vehicle Company. Then, in 1899, he moved the firm to the town that was to become known as 'Motor City' – Detroit. Now called the Olds Motor Works, it was here that several prototype cars were constructed.

# Curved Dash Oldsmobile

Unfortunately, a catastrophic fire in March 1901 destroyed all but one of Old's creations. Heroically pulled from the flames, this one car was all that Olds had left to work with. He claimed that even the blueprints had been lost and that new ones had to be drawn up from the single survivor. Fortune appeared to have played a part, because this was to become the Curved Dash Oldsmobile – and a runaway success. The role of the fire took on almost mythical status, although it must be added that a reliable source stated that

the blueprints did survive, and that there were 334 advance orders for the car before the fire, so production was already assured. Olds was plainly an excellent public relations man!

With its premises in ruins, it was essential to get the car into production quickly to keep the company afloat. Olds made the clever decision to contract out the manufacture of his car's component parts: engines, transmissions and the skimpy little bodies were all made by other companies, and then assembled by Olds. He can be credited with single-handedly inventing the production line, with the cars rolled along while different groups of workers assembled the various parts of the vehicle, although Henry Ford would later take the idea much further.

The car was simple and fairly typical of American cars of the time. It had a wooden frame with long leaf springs running the length of it and providing front and rear suspension. High ground clearance meant it could cope with the rough roads of the time. The engine was a single cylinder 1,565cc unit utilising a two-speed epicyclic to achieve a heady 500rpm at its top speed of 20mph, and was said to provide, in the parlance of the time, 'one chug per telegraph pole'.

By the time production ceased in 1905, nearly 19,000 had been built. This made Oldsmobile the largest motor manufacturer in the world from 1903 to 1905. Many survive, and around 30 regularly take part in the London to Brighton run.

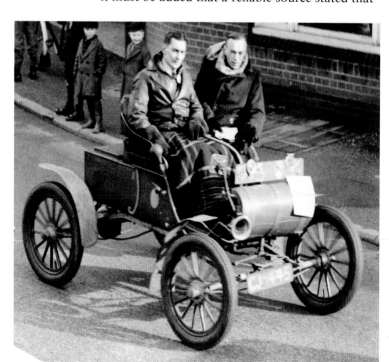

## Specifications

| | |
|---|---|
| Production dates | 1901-1905 |
| Manufactured units | 18,525 |
| Engine type | Single-cylinder, rear-mounted |
| Engine size | 1,565cc |
| Maximum power | 5bhp |
| Transmission | 2-speed epicyclic |
| Top speed | 20mph |
| 0-60 mph time | N/A |
| Country of origin | USA |

*15 million Tin Lizzies put America and the world on wheels*

In 1904, Henry Ford became the fastest man on earth when he drove his crude 'Arrow' across the frozen Lake St Clair at 91.37mph. It provided invaluable publicity for his first production car, the 'A', which debuted soon after, although the experience was so terrifying that it robbed Ford of any further interest in speed. By 1908, Ford was running through the letters of alphabet in naming his cars, and got as far as the Model T – arguably the most important car in history.

# Model T Ford

In 1902, Ford stated his intention to 'build a car for the great multitudes'. By 1906, he was already America's largest manufacturer, but the T was to revolutionize the industry.'

The four-cylinder 2,884cc engine had a detachable cylinder head, which was a new idea, but otherwise the T was fairly typical of its day, with high ground clearance and a two-speed gearbox.

Introduced in October 1908, it carried the rather hefty price tag of $850. Henry was under pressure to bring the price down, but refused to compromise on quality, so another way to reduce costs had to be found – and the answer came in the form of the world's first moving production line. Assembly time fell from 12 hours and 28 minutes to a remarkable 1 hour and 33 minutes. As production soared, the price dropped to an all-time low in 1925 – an extraordinarily cheap $290.

Ford paid his workers well and they worked hard as a result. Production numbers were phenomenal, rising to nearly two million cars per year. The

'Tin Lizzie' lasted all the way through to 1927, by which time it had sold 15,007,033 units. It took until the 1970s for this number to be exceeded by the VW Beetle.

The Model T changed remarkably little during its 19-year run, although the brass radiator went in 1917 and its styling was modernized. The cars were lowered in 1923, no doubt as roads improved, and then again in 1926. This was the year that also saw the introduction of a choice of colours aside from the original black.

Model Ts were designed in a range of styles – from touring, runabout and coupé to two- and four-door sedans, not to mention delivery and commercial vehicles. Racing on banked board tracks was popular across the US in the 1920s, and cut-down Model Ts were a popular racer.

As the car of choice for everyone from the man on the street to Laurel and Hardy on the silver screen, The Tin Lizzie integrated itself into the American psyche like no other automobile.

## Specifications

| | |
|---|---|
| Production dates | 1908-1927 |
| Manufactured units | 15,007,033 |
| Engine type | 4-cylinder side-valve front-mounted |
| Engine size | 2,884cc |
| Maximum power | 20bhp at 1,800rpm |
| Transmission | 2-speed epicyclic |
| Top speed | 42mph |
| 0-60 mph time | N/A |
| Country of origin | USA |

*Available in any shade... as long as it's black. Henry Ford found that black paint dried faster, speeding up production*

*Generations of British motorists learned to drive in the charming little Seven*

Although primarily an engineer, Herbert Austin was no less an entrepreneur. By 1906, he had formed the Austin Motor Company, and by 1917 his famous factory at Longbridge was Britain's biggest motor works, due in part to large-scale war contracts. Austin was knighted for his services to the nation and became a Lord in 1936.

Impressed by Henry Ford's methods with the Model T, Austin implemented a single-model

# Austin Seven

policy and a production line. Unfortunately, the large 20hp model was not a success, and Austin escaped bankruptcy and a merger with General Motors by the skin of his teeth.

Deciding that cheaper cars were a safer bet, Austin introduced the Twelve in 1921, following it up in 1922 with the diminutive Seven.

The Seven was a simple little motor car. A small 747cc four-cylinder side-valve engine produced a modest 10bhp. This was set in a rather spindly A-shaped chassis. Its flexibility, combined with soft leaf springs front and rear, gave the Seven 'interesting' handling. It had four wheel brakes, but they were tiny and operated by stretchy cables. A top speed of only 42mph saved many an inexperienced driver from a grisly end. Untold numbers of Brits learned to drive in the Seven, and this, combined with its enormous charm, gives it a unique place in British motoring history.

The Seven appeared in numerous forms, including open tourers, two-seat convertibles, saloons and

vans, with names like Chummy, Ruby and Pearl. There were also sporting models, the Ulster being the most sought after. Sevens were the first cars bodied by Swallow Sidecars, which became SS, in turn becoming Jaguar. A whole cottage industry emerged, transforming Sevens into little competition cars, and there are innumerable Sevens still racing. The factory even built a twin-cam supercharged racing car that circulated the Brooklands track at amazing speeds in the 1930s.

The Seven went international, being built under licence in France, Germany and the US. In Germany, it became the first ever BMW car, the Dixi. In the US it was built by American Austin, but Americans were suspicious of such a tiny car and bankruptcy became inevitable. A little later, the Seven re-emerged as the American Bantam, but even then it didn't sell well.

By the time it bowed out in 1939, over 375,000 Sevens had been built. The later models were more modern in their manners than the earlier ones, but any Seven remains a great car for spanner-happy enthusiasts who aren't in a hurry.

## Specifications

| | |
|---|---|
| Production dates | 1922-1939 |
| Manufactured units | 375,000+ |
| Engine type | 4-cylinder side-valve front-mounted |
| Engine size | 747cc |
| Maximum power | 10-14bhp (more for racing versions) |
| Transmission | 3-speed (early cars); 4-speed (later cars) |
| Top speed | 42mph |
| 0-60 mph time | N/A |
| Country of origin | UK |

*Swallow Sidecars built bodies for Austin Sevens that most definitely had ideas above their station. Swallow sidecars became SS, and of course after WW2 they hanged their name to Jaguar*

*Famous victories at Le Mans for the Bentley Boys made the 3.0 ltr a legend*

Ettore Bugatti, who created the Bugatti car, famously remarked that Bentleys were 'the world's fastest lorries'. He had a point. Walter Owen Bentley had trained as a locomotive engineer and a certain weight and solidity were common to all his designs.

During the Great War, he designed two rotary aero engines for the Admiralty, and by 1919 he had the prototype of his 3.0-litre car displayed at the Olympia show in London, not that far from

# Bentley 3.0 ltr

his Cricklewood factory. It took another two years, however, before he could offer it for sale.

The Bentley was fairly conventional, even if its four-cylinder engine did have the modern configuration of four valves per cylinder operated by an overhead camshaft. This was mounted in a massively constructed chassis, and all of WO's four- and six-cylinder cars shared these features.

Sales were slow and racing success was needed to promote the car. An entry into the inaugural Le Mans 24 Hour in 1923 netted fourth place. Drivers Duff and Clement returned in 1924 with the new Speed Model, and they won.

Both 1925 and 1926 brought only retirements and so WO decided to develop a more powerful car – the 4.5-litre. Always strapped for cash, WO persuaded diamond millionaire and racing driver Woolf Barnato to take the chair of the company and finance the new model. Barnato was one of the 'Bentley Boys', extremely wealthy young men who raced Bentleys, the most famous of their set being 'Tim' Birkin.

1927 is perhaps the most famous of all Le Mans 24 hours, and it was the 3.0-litre's finest hour. Three 3.0-litres and one 4.5-litre car were entered, and were likely favourites. The big car took the lead, but three of the Bentleys became involved in a terrible six-car pile up at White Horse corner. Miraculously, nobody was killed, and Sammy Davis managed to limp his 3.0-litre back to the pits. It was very badly damaged, but after half an hour of repairs the mangled car was back on the track. Davis and his co-driver Benjafield took a victory worthy of the pages of 'Boys Own' magazine.

There were further victories in the French race in 1928, 1929 and 1930, but they couldn't save Bentley from bankruptcy, and in 1931 the company was bought by Rolls Royce.

The 'Cricklewood' Bentleys remain the most archetypal of vintage cars, and more British than fish and chips or Buckingham Palace.

### Specifications

| | |
|---|---|
| Production dates | 1921-1927 |
| Manufactured units | 1,633 |
| Engine type | 4-cylinder 16-valve front-mounted |
| Engine size | 2,996cc |
| Maximum power | 80-90 bhp |
| Transmission | 4-speed |
| Top speed | 80mph |
| 0-60 mph time | N/A |
| Country of origin | UK |

At the 1927 Le Mans 24-hour race there was a terrible pile up at White House corner. The Bentley of Davis and Benjafield was involved, but somehow it limped back to the pits. Although it took half an hour to straighten out, it went on to score an heroic victory

*The exquisite little blue cars from Molsheim won literally hundreds of races, including the first Monaco Grand Prix*

Ettore Bugatti was an Italian who built the most celebrated cars ever to wear French racing blue. He was perhaps an artist first and an engineer second. Together with his son Jean, he produced what were quite simply some of the most fabulous automobiles ever made.

Ettore set up in the town of Molsheim in Alsace and began trading on 1st January, 1910. The town had been German, but after a war spent designing

# Bugatti Type 35/35B

aero engines in Paris, Ettore returned to a French town. His successful Brescia model, based on the pre-war Type 13, became a respected racing car, with many victories to its name.

In 1922, Ettore designed the engine for the Type 30 – a 2.0-litre straight eight with one exhaust and two inlet valves per cylinder, driven by an overhead camshaft. In 1924, a development of this engine was used to power the new Type 35 competition car. It was a Grand Prix car, but had

two seats so that it was capable of carrying a riding mechanic.

Every detail was meticulously conceived, designed and manufactured. The aim was to save weight, but the result was an exquisite automobile. At a time when many cars ran on wooden wheels and sports cars all had wire wheels, Ettore created beautiful eight-spoke cast aluminium wheels, with integral brake drums. The engine was also a work of art, with a simple unadorned design.

The Type 35 was a huge success, and as it developed it became faster and faster. The Type 35B was the ultimate version, with a 2.3-litre engine fed by a supercharger. In 1926 it was capable of reaching 125mph, and in that year it won the World Championship. By the end of the 1920s Bugattis had won more races – including the first Monaco Grand Prix – than any other manufacturer, and Type 35Bs were credited with winning an average of 14 races per week! The Type 35 was developed into the 51, with twin overhead cams and yet more power, but by that time German teams ruled the Grand Prix roost.

Today, the Type 35B is one of the world's most valuable cars – and if you've seen one racing, you'll know why. The music of the unsilenced straight eight, overlaid with the high-pitched scream of the supercharger, is never forgotten. In its day, it was described as 'tearing calico'. In reality, it's the sound of mechanical genius.

### Specifications

| | |
|---|---|
| Production dates | 1926-1928 |
| Manufactured units | 45 |
| Engine type | Straight 8 supercharged |
| Engine size | 2,262cc |
| Maximum power | 138bhp |
| Transmission | 4-speed |
| Top speed | 125mph |
| 0-60 mph time | N/A |
| Country of origin | France |

*The Type 35 and 35B Bugattis were phenomenally successful competition cars. In the late 1920s it was said that they averaged 14 race wins per week!*

*For Clarke Gable and Gary Cooper, only a Duesenberg would do*

Fred and August Duesenberg were German born, but came to America in the 1880s. In 1913, they began manufacturing engines at the Duesenberg Motor Company, and in 1917 the first car bearing their names was released. Despite undertaking aero engine contracts during the Great War, the brothers' passion was for racing, and after the war they moved their business to Indianapolis. In 1920, one of their cars reached 156mph – a new world record that was never officially recognised.

# Duesenberg Model J

Bodies were designed and built by the best coach builders, but Cord wanted a stronger, more individual identity, and so employed the gifted designer Gordon Buehrig, just 25 at the time. His fabulous designs were executed by coachbuilders such as Derham, Murphy, Brewster and Le Baron, and the results were some of the most opulent and extravagant automobiles ever seen.

Fred and Augie's first road car was the Model A of 1920. It was expensive, but this was America's first straight eight, and the first with hydraulic brakes. Another first occured in 1921, when a Model A won the French Grand Prix – the first victory for an American car in Europe.

Unfortunately, the brothers went bust, and in 1926 the company was bought by entrepreneur Errett Cord, who owned Auburn. He announced his intention to build the world's most expensive car, releasing the Model J in December 1928.

The engine was a 7.0-litre straight eight with four valves per cylinder and twin overhead camshafts. The chassis came in two lengths, and this alone cost $8,500. Once bodied, the whole thing would have cost around $17,000 – four times the price of the most expensive Cadillac!

This was not a great time to be selling expensive automobiles, as the Wall Street crash left few people able to afford them, but in 1932 the SJ was released. Built on a new shorter chassis, it had a supercharged engine reputed to make 320bhp, capable of pushing it up to 140mph. Only 36 people were rich enough to buy one. There was also a 400bph SSJ, bought only by movie stars.

The company staggered on, but in 1937 Cord was investigated by the Securities and Exchange Commission. He was put out of business, and the Duesenberg factory was eventually sold on to a truck company.

Duesenbergs are the most treasured of all American cars, and on the rare occasions they change hands, it's usually behind closed doors for undisclosed – and unbelievable – sums of money.

## Specifications

| | |
|---|---|
| Production dates | 1928-1935 |
| Manufactured units | 470 |
| Engine type | Straight 8 twin cam DOHC; SJ/SSJ supercharged |
| Engine size | 6,882cc |
| Maximum power | 265bhp (J); 320bhp (SJ); 400bhp (SSJ) |
| Transmission | 4-speed |
| Top speed | 115mph (J); 140mph (SJ) |
| 0-60 mph time | 8.6 seconds (J) |
| Country of origin | USA |

*The Model J Duesenbergs were the most fabulous American cars ever made... and so they should have been, as they were the highest-priced cars in the world*

*With his first V8
Henry Ford really did
bring power to the people*

After 15,000,000 Tin Lizzies came the Model A. Within 18 months of its 1928 launch, there were 2,000,000 of them on America's roads. It had a four cylinder engine, and although a little dearer, Chevrolet could give you six. Then came the Depression, during which sales fell so low that, in July 1931, Ford had to lay off 75,000 of his workers. Ford knew that something radical was needed to win back sales.

Released on April 2nd 1932, there were 14 V8 models to choose from. The styling was sleek, modern and very attractive. Priced from $460 to $650, with an 80mph top speed they were faster than most sports cars. Ford won back sales from the competition, but the Depression meant that only 232,125 cars were built in 1932.

# '32 Ford

Since 1930, his best engineers had been working on a low cost V8 engine that was to be the Ford secret sales weapon. Cadillac had built a V8 as early as 1914, and other makes were also V8 powered. These engines were expensive to manufacture, being made up of several separate castings. Ford's plan was to cast it in one, with the crankshaft also a single casting. The technology didn't come cheap, and rebuilding the forge at the Rouge River plant cost $55,000,000. However, when production got underway, his factory was able to turn out 3,000 engines every day.

With some developments, the 'flat head' V8 engine powered Fords up until the war, as well as Bren gun carriers, armoured cars and boats during the war, and French and British Fords well into the 1950s.

The 3,621cc side valve engine had huge tuning potential, and it was the 1932, or 'Deuce', which got hot rodding going all on its own. A few stripped-out, hopped-up '32s would make their way to the dry lake beds in California for illegal races. When GIs returned after WW2, the Deuce was a cheap way to go fast, and the whole hot rod and drag racing scene took off. Tuning the flat head and V8s that followed grew into a massive industry of its own.

Immortalised by the Beach Boys in 'Little Deuce Coupé', and by George Lucas as John Milner's car in 'American Graffiti', even now the '32 remains the world's favourite hot rod.

### Specifications

| | |
|---|---|
| Production dates | 1932 |
| Manufactured units | 232,125 |
| Engine type | Side-valve V8 |
| Engine size | 3,621cc |
| Maximum power | 65bhp |
| Transmission | 3-speed synchromesh |
| Top speed | 80mph |
| 0-50 mph time | 12 seconds |
| Country of origin | USA |

*Charismatic or caricature; the K cars were the ultimate embodiment of 1930s style*

The Mercedes marque had become associated with supercharging in the late 1920s with the mighty SS and SSK sports cars. These were stripped down racers where form obeyed function – something that could never be said of the K cars.

On paper, their specification followed that of the Mercedes Grand Prix cars – straight eight supercharged engines and all independent suspension – but that's where the similarity ended.

# Mercedes 500K/540K

bursts. It was renowned for making a fearsome scream, although there are those who say that this had more to do with the perception of increased performance than any extra horse power involved. With that blower going, fuel consumption dropped to 8mpg!

Unusually for exclusive cars of the time, nearly all of the K cars were bodied at the factory. The four-seater cabriolet B and the two-seater cabriolet A are highly prized, but the Special Roadster is the supreme embodiment. It has more curves and chrome than almost any car in history; the epitome of 'erotic' aesthetics in car design.

The cars were bought by the world's richest men – an Indian Maharajah even used his to hunt tigers. Unfortunately, we can't pretend that the charisma of these cars did not appeal to the Nazi high command. There was even an order for 20 armoured versions of the 540K for the more jittery Third Reich officers.

The styling of the K cars may be overblown and even verge on caricature, but the Special Roadster is one of the most recognised cars ever. Seven decades later, its image is still selling Mercedes.

The first of the line was the 380 in 1933. Although it was blown like its big brothers, it was felt to be underpowered. In 1934 came the 500K, and a legend that lives to this day was born.

The 500K was built to be magnificent. Its 5.0-litre engine was moved 7in back in the chassis to allow the radiator grill to be set right back behind the axle line. The bonnet was impossibly long, though this was partially excused by the length of that engine. There were many body styles, designed and built in-house at Sindlefingen, and all were breathtaking. Performance was good, but not quite up to expectations.

In 1936 came the 540K with 180bhp. This was produced only when the supercharger was engaged, which could be done only in short

## Specifications

| | |
|---|---|
| Production dates | 1934-1936 (500K); 1936-1939 (540K) |
| Manufactured units | 354 (500K); 406 (540K) |
| Engine type | Straight 8 OHV supercharged |
| Engine size | 5,018cc (500K); 54,01cc (540K) |
| Maximum power | (with supercharger) 160bhp (500K); 180bhp (540K) |
| Transmission | 3-speed + overdrive/ 4-speed/4-speed + |
| Top speed | 105mph |
| 0-50 mph time | 16 seconds |
| Country of origin | Germany |

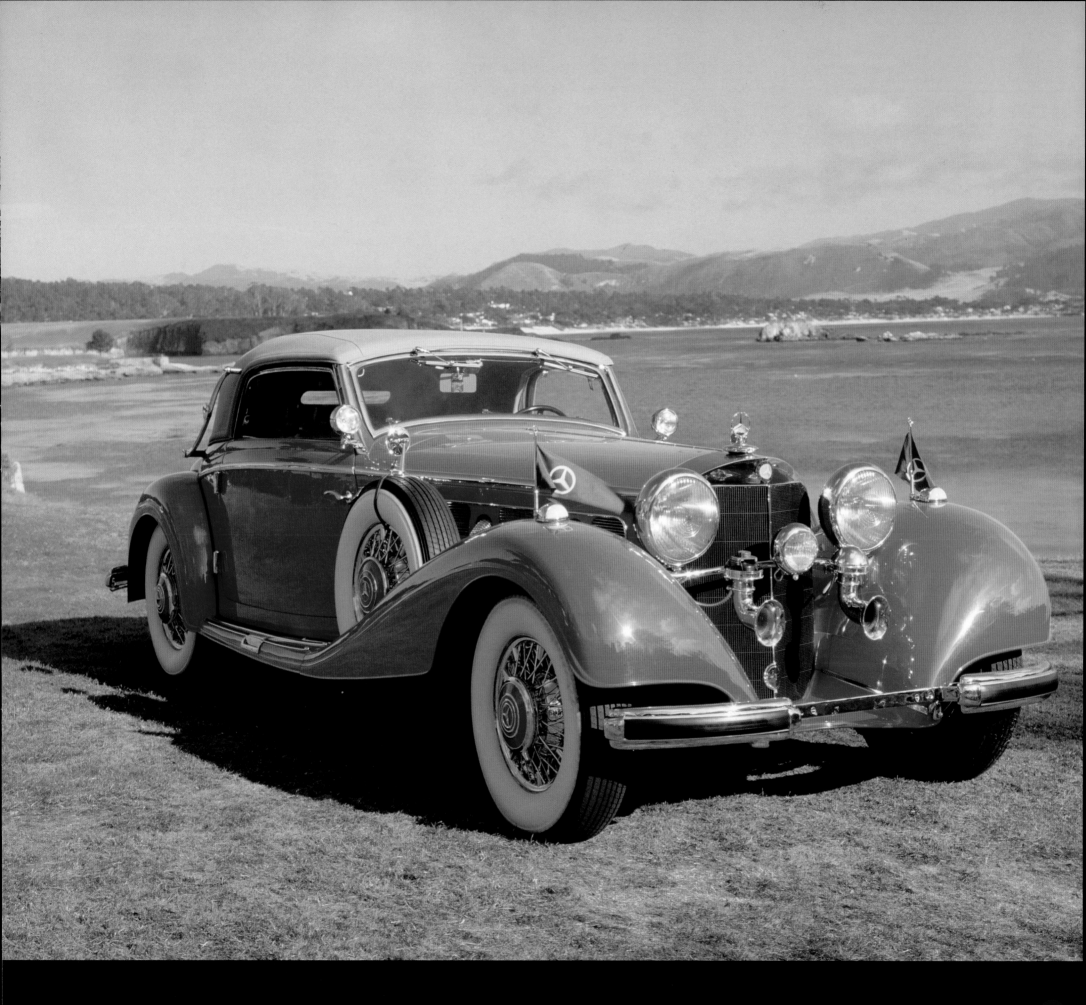

*Even when clothed in coachwork that was relatively restrained, and wearing sombre black paintwork, the K cars could manage a flamboyance that few could approach*

*Genius Buehrig's makeover creates an all-time classic design*

Auburn is the town in Indiana where brothers Frank and Morris Eckhart established their automobile business in 1903. Starting with simple single-cylinder devices, they had progressed to a six-cylinder car by 1912. In truth, their cars were undistinguished and pricey, and by 1924 they were failing, with 700 unsold cars on their hands.

Errett Lobban Cord had made and lost his fortune three times over by the age of 24, but by 1924,

# Auburn 851/ 852 Speedster

his genius for selling seemed to have cemented his wealth. Taken on to run the ailing Auburn company, he immediately spruced up the unsold cars with jazzy colours – and, sure enough, they sold. He soon bought the company, becoming its dynamic president in 1926 at the age of 32.

A new Auburn range was introduced, the most important being a straight eight. The engine was built by aero engine makers Lycoming, which Cord had also bought. In fact, by 1929 his Cord Corporation controlled over 150 companies!

In 1928 came the Speedster. Cord always believed that if a car looked good it would sell – and the Speedster looked great. By 1931, all Auburns were straight eight powered, and it became their best ever year. However, from there things began to slide. In 1934, the Speedster received a makeover, but it wasn't enough. What the Speedster needed was a complete redesign, but unfortunately there simply wasn't the money for an all-new car.

The young designer Gordon Buehrig had been doing amazing work for the Cord Corporation, including creating the 'Duesenberg look'. Given the job of sorting out the Speedster, but with 100 bodies in stock needing to be used up, his redesign could only be superficial. Taking the 1928 car he created a new rear end, hood, grill and fenders. With this he managed to fashion what appeared to be a completely new car, and one of the all time great automotive shapes. It was introduced in 1935 as the 851, and then again in 1936 as the 852, although little more than the badge had changed between the two.

The 851's simple side valve straight eight was supercharged to 150bhp, but it was essentially a cheap car in a fancy suit. At $2,245, it should have sold, but these were hard times in America, and in 1937 Auburn went under.

With their cut price underpinnings forgotten, the 851 and 852 Cords are now held up as the pinnacle of art deco automotive styling.

## Specifications

| | |
|---|---|
| Production dates | 851 1935; 852 1936-1937 |
| Manufactured units | 6,850 (851/852, all styles); approx 600 (Speedster) |
| Engine type | Straight 8 supercharged |
| Engine size | 4,585cc |
| Maximum power | 150bhp |
| Transmission | 3-speed + 2-speed (6-speed) |
| Top speed | 103mph |
| 0-50 mph time | 15 seconds |
| Country of origin | USA |

*Buehrig managed to fashion what appeared to be a completely new car, and one of the all-time great automotive shapes*

*The last word in 1930s bespoke engineering*

The 'best cars in the world' came about through the partnership of engineer Henry Royce and salesman Charles Rolls. Their 40/50 model of 1906, known as the Silver Ghost, was certainly worthy of this accolade: the famously silent Ghost was made right up until 1926, with many built at their US factory in Springfield, Massachusetts.

During the Great War, Rolls-Royce had begun to built V12 aero engines, though it was not until

# Rolls-Royce Phantom III

1936 that this configuration of engine would appear in one on their cars. This meant that neither Royce nor Rolls were to see this ultimate development of their car: Rolls was the first Englishman to die in an air crash in 1910 and Royce died in 1933.

In 1926 came the Phantom I, with a new overhead valve 7,668cc six-cylinder engine. For 1929 it evolved into the Phantom II. There was also a smaller 20hp model, which developed into the 20/25 and the 25/30. It was the Phantom III, however, that was to be the pinnacle of pre-WW2 automotive engineering.

The aircraft and ship engines produced by Rolls-Royce were a major influence on the engine of the PIII, a 7,340cc overhead valve V12. Cadillac had tried to go one up with a V16, but it was a simple side-valve device, and not in the same engineering league as the PIII. The advantages of the V12 layout were sublime smoothness and considerable power: Rolls-Royce were always coy about power outputs, simply stating that they were 'adequate'. In fact, the V12 made something like 170bhp, which was more than adequate.

The PIII also had far more modern suspension than its predecessors. The independent front suspension used coil springs and wishbones, as developed by General Motors.

Unsurprisingly, the PIII was expensive. Not until after the war did RR build their own bodies, so having purchased the chassis a person then had to take it to their favourite coachbuilder. In the US, a complete car would have cost around $15,000 – the same amount that would have bought five Cadillac 75s!

Hostilities of 1939 halted production, which meant that the V12 never reached its development potential, and the era of hand-built bespoke engineering came to a close.

Incidentally, a Phantom III should never be referred to as a 'Rolls': any pre-war Rolls-Royce is more appropriately referred to as a 'Royce'.

### Specifications

| Specifications | |
| --- | --- |
| Production dates | 1936-1939 |
| Manufactured units | 710 |
| Engine type | V12, pushrod operated overhead valve |
| Engine size | 7,340cc |
| Maximum power | 170bph |
| Transmission | 4-speed synchromesh |
| Top speed | Approx 92mph |
| 0-50 mph time | N/A |
| Country of origin | UK |

*The streamlined Cord car and Cord the man: both American icons*

It it said that Errett Lobban Cord knew nothing about cars – except how to sell them. He made more than half a dozen fortunes in his life (and lost a few of them), yet Cord is best remembered through the cars that bore his name.

Having bought and turned around both Auburn and Duesenberg, in 1929 he launched his own car. The Cord L-29 was radical in that it had front wheel drive. The Miller front-drive racing cars

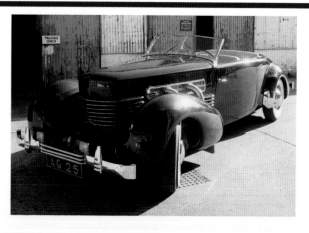

# Cord 810/812

had been beating the Duesenbergs at Indianapolis, and Cord wanted it for his road car.

The car looked terrific, but transmission problems, a high price tag and a dull Lycoming engine meant that it was a flop. Something much better was needed.

In December 1935, the new Cord 810 debuted at the New York show. It was a sensation. There was still front wheel drive, but a far more sophisticated design. There was a also a new V8 engine, with the option of supercharging up to 190bhp, pushing the Cord to 110 mph. Gear changing was achieved via electric solenoids controlled by a tiny lever. All told, it was a completely new car – and one that drove a whole lot better than the L-29. In fact, its cornering ability was in a different class to anything else on the market.

Designer Gordon Buehrig had created a stylish masterpiece. Construction was unitary, with no separate chassis, which allowed the car to be very low to the ground. Headlights were hidden in the fenders, while louvers extended round the front and back to the doors, with a 'coffin nose' hood above. The interior was also spectacular, with an aircraft-inspired dashboard.

Convertible, phaeton and two sedan models were constructed. Unusually, it is arguably the sedans that are the most stunning of the lot, with lines that were cleaner than anything on American or European roads at the time.

For 1937, the Cords were retitled 812s. It was to be their last year. Cord had gone to England in 1934 due to investigations into his business practices. In 1937, a bill was filed against him and Cord production stopped.

These were hard times in the US, and sales of the revolutionary Cord were never strong, but Buehrig's shape is now recognised as one of the most beautiful and influential automotive designs of all time.

## Specifications

| | |
|---|---|
| Production dates | 1936-1937 |
| Manufactured units | 2,320 |
| Engine type | V8 side-valve, optional supercharger |
| Engine size | 4,719cc |
| Maximum power | 115bhp (190bhp supercharged) |
| Transmission | 4-speed, electric gear selection, front-wheel drive |
| Top speed | 91mph (110mph supercharged) |
| 0-50 mph time | N/A |
| Country of origin | USA |

*Designer Gordon Buehrig gave the Cord some of the most original and beautiful lines ever seen. It was no less imaginative under the skin, with front-wheel drive and electric gear selection*

*The GIs' transport of choice
that went from being a legend
to an institution*

In 1940, America was still some way from entering the war in Europe, but there was enough concern for the US Quartermaster Corps to issue an invitation in July to 135 US manufacturers, asking them to submit prototypes for a general purpose vehicle. There was a list of requirements including an 80in wheelbase, 50mph top speed and a very optimistic limit on weight. This put off many contenders, and it was the tiny Bantam company that met the deadline.

further 15,000 to the Willys design. Poor old Bantam got to supply trailers, and never built another car, despite their initial success.

America entered the war and demand soared. At their peak, a Jeep was leaving the Willys production line every 90 seconds. By the end of the war, over 350,000 Jeeps had been supplied to US, British and Russian forces, making a huge contribution to the Allied victory.

# Jeep

Bantam had been making Austin Sevens under licence, but were not doing well. They enlisted freelance engineer Karl K Probst, and a prototype and drawings were duly delivered in an incredible seven weeks. Although overweight, it was considered to be a success. Ford and Willys Overland also submitted. They had access to the Bantam, and so their designs were very similar. Seventy vehicles from each company were made, after which the three companies were asked to build 1,500 vehicles for evaluation.

The Willys had the best engine, and was the best value at $739. The design was standardised, and due to concerns about Bantam's lack of capacity, the contract went to Willys. Sixteen thousand were ordered, but even Willys were unlikely to meet demand, so Ford were asked to build a

The Jeep's 60bhp side-valve four-cylinder engine gave it a top speed of over 60mph. It had a three-speed synchromesh gearbox connected to a high/low transfer box and four-wheel drive. With minimal overhangs and good ground clearance, it took seriously rough terrain to halt its progress, and ended up being used as everything from a gun platform, to radio car, reconnaissance vehicle and ambulance. It was easy to drive, simple to maintain, and – most of all – extremely tough.

Willys went on to build a civilian version, and the Jeep has been an institution ever since. Others copied the formula, and the British Land Rover went on sale as early as 1948.

As to where that name came from – GP, for 'general purpose', is the most likely explanation.

## Specifications

| | |
|---|---|
| Production dates | 1941 to present |
| Manufactured units | 350,000 (1941-1945) |
| Engine type | 4-cylinder side valve |
| Engine size | 2,199cc |
| Maximum power | 60bhp |
| Transmission | 3-speed sychromesh + 2-speed transfer box, 4-wheel drive |
| Top speed | 65mph |
| 0-50 mph time | N/A |
| Country of origin | USA |

*In the Jeep was a rightness found only when form follows function and purpose so completely. A very similar vehicle to the WW2 Jeep is still made in India*

*Old-fashioned and not very fast, but post-war America fell in love with the little MG*

The 'Bullnose' was William Morris' first car in 1913. The cars were sold from a converted stable in Oxford, not far from the Abingdon works. This became known as Morris Garages, and from 1922 the retail side of the business was run by Cecil Kimber. It was Kimber who was to create the MG marque, MG standing for 'Morris Garages'.

The first MGs soon appeared, but it wasn't until 1929 that MG really got moving with the Midget.

# MG TC

Based on the Morris Minor, it had a lively and modern overhead cam 850cc engine.

In 1930, 1,000 MGs were built, and success meant moving over to Abingdon. This was also the year that the famous slogan, 'safety fast', was coined. MGs were doing well on the race tracks, beating arch rivals Austin in the Brooklands Double Twelve – Britain's equivalent of the Le Mans 24 Hour – amongst many other victories.

1933 saw the creation of the J2 Midget, and this was to establish the styling of MGs all the way through to the 1950s: a radiator well set back,

flowing wings, cut down doors, a fuel tank on the back and a folding windscreen.

In 1934 came the TA Midget, which was based on the Morris Ten saloon, and which used its pushrod 1,292cc engine. This seemed a retrograde step after the overhead cam unit of its predecessor. However, it was larger, so power did not suffer, and neither did sales.

In fact, the engine was more flexible, and, with softer suspension and modern hydraulic brakes, it was an altogether easier car to drive. The traditional MG styling had reached its perfection, and it is still many people's idea of what a real sports car should be.

With a revised engine it became the TB – at which point war stopped play. After 1945, there was a huge hunger for new cars, especially sports cars as a source of fun after the grim years of fighting. There had been no development of new cars since 1939, so most manufacturers dusted off their old models as best they could. The TC came to the market in 1946, and MG couldn't make enough of them. Little had changed from the TB: it remained archaic but extremely charming. Thousands of units went to America, starting the US love affair with British sports cars that has endured to this day.

**Specifications**

| | |
|---|---|
| Production dates | 1946-1949 |
| Manufactured units | 10,000 |
| Engine type | 4-cylinder pushrod OHV |
| Engine size | 1,250cc |
| Maximum power | 54bhp |
| Transmission | 4-speed synchromesh |
| Top speed | 78mph |
| 0-50 mph time | N/A |
| Country of origin | UK |

*These were the vehicles that started the US' enduring love affair with British sports cars*

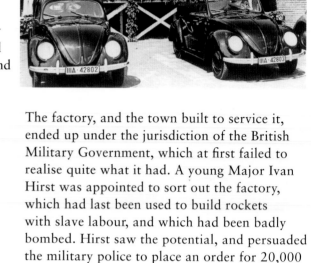

*The inimitable Bug has the strangest and longest story of any motor car in history*

On July 30th, 2003, Beetle number 21,529,464 left the Puebla factory in Mexico. It was the very last one. The story of the world's most successful car had started an incredible 70 years earlier – and it's one of the most remarkable in the business.

Hitler is often credited with inventing the Beetle, but it wasn't really so. The idea came from Dr Ferdinand Porsche, and was brought to Hitler's attention in 1933, the year that he became

# VW Beetle

chancellor. It was on June 22, 1934 that Porsche secured a contract to build a prototype for the 'people's car'.

There is much discussion over who contributed what to the design, but Czech Hans Ledwinka, from the Tatra company, is thought by some to have had much to do with it. By 1934 there was also a very Beetle-esque rear-engine Mercedes on the market.

With assistance from Mercedes Benz, three cars were built in 1936, and a further 30 pre-production cars in 1937. In 1938, Hitler laid the foundation stone of the factory near Hanover where the car was to be built. It was to be called the 'KdF-Wagen', or, 'strength through joy car'. The new factory spent the war making weapons and military vehicles, but in 1945 the tooling for the KdF-Wagen had survived.

The factory, and the town built to service it, ended up under the jurisdiction of the British Military Government, which at first failed to realise quite what it had. A young Major Ivan Hirst was appointed to sort out the factory, which had last been used to build rockets with slave labour, and which had been badly bombed. Hirst saw the potential, and persuaded the military police to place an order for 20,000 vehicles. He scrounged steel and supplies, and by 1946, 1,000 cars a month were being built. In 1949, the renamed Wolfsburg town and factory were handed over to the new West German government.

VW promoted the little car in the US, and against all preconceptions the Americans took the Bug to their heart, buying them in their millions.

The tiny 1,131cc engine grew in size and power, while the split rear window became one, and got bigger. Eventually, the windscreen became curved and the torsion bar front suspension gave way to modern struts. And yet the Beetle's character never really changed.

In 1972, it overtook the Model T Ford's record for production numbers, and it seems unlikely that any car will ever exceed the VW's 21.5 million examples built over its 57 years.

## Specifications

| | |
|---|---|
| Production dates | 1946-2003 |
| Manufactured units | 21,529,464 |
| Engine type | Flat 4, air-cooled, rear-mounted |
| Engine size | 1,131cc-1,584cc |
| Maximum power | 25bhp-50bhp |
| Transmission | 4-speed synchromesh |
| Top speed | 62mph-82mph |
| 0-60 mph time | 17.1 seconds (1,303-1,584cc) |
| Country of origin | Germany |

*...against all preconceptions the Americans took the Bug to their hearts, buying them in their millions*

*Race track domination and fabulous looks couldn't save Hudson*

# Hudson Hornet

Hudson had been around since 1908 and, at times in the 1930s, had risen as high as number five in US sales, but remained a relatively small fish in an extremely big pond, and so life was never easy.

The war brought the production of Helldiver planes and parts for B29s, but following VJ Day in 1945, Hudson made enough cars to regain fifth place. The cars created between 1945 and 1947 were based on old designs, but for 1948 it had an all-new car. These were the 'Step Down' Hudsons, and the Commodore models made money for the old firm.

The nickname came from the way in which the main chassis members ran around the perimeter of the car, allowing the floor to be stepped down inside. Not only did this make the car extremely low, it also made it exceptionally safe.

There was a new engine as well. The Super Six was a side-valve 4,294cc unit, and was only marginally less powerful than Hudson's straight eight. By 1951 it had become rebranded as the 5,048cc Hornet engine.

The Hornet looked much like the Commodore, but with a new grill. The lines were sensational and, while performance from the 145bhp motor was excellent, there was potential for more and the car became a tuner's favourite. Marshall Teague said he could get 112mph out of a car certified as stock by the racing authorities. The Hudson engineers developed 'severe usage' parts, which were really racing equipment. In 1953, the Twin H Power carburettor setup was offered. The ultimate '7-X' racing engine could make 210bhp.

Teague raced the Hornet in AAA and NASCAR stock-car events from 1951 and was simply invincible through to 1954, winning 12 out of 13 races in the 1952 AAA season. As late as 1955, after Step Down production had finished, the Hornet was still winning races.

The trouble was that the Hornet's modern unitary construction and fabulous lines made it impossible to restyle year to year in the way that most manufacturers did: all its designers could do was fiddle with the trim. It also hurt sales that however good the Hudson engine was, it wasn't a V8. Profits fell, and in 1954 came a merger with Nash – really more of a takeover by their rival. The 1955 Hudson used a Nash body, and was disparagingly referred to as a 'Hash'.

## Specifications

| | |
|---|---|
| Production dates | 1951-1953 |
| Manufactured units | 106,785 |
| Engine type | 6-cylinder side valve |
| Engine size | 5,048cc |
| Maximum power | 145bhp, Twin H Power 160bhp |
| Transmission | 3-speed manual, with options of overdrive and Drive-Master semi- automatic; Hydra-Matic automatic gearbox optional |
| Top speed | 105mph |
| 0-60 mph time | 12-14 seconds |
| Country of origin | USA |

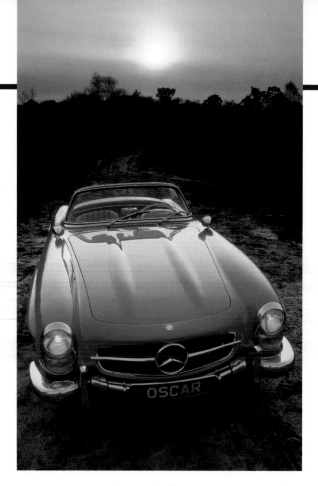

*Could the 300SL be the world's most desired automobile?*

The 300SL is seen by most as the greatest car Mercedes Benz ever built. And yet, without some very strong external persuasion, it would never have come into being.

Daimler Benz was all but obliterated by Allied bombing during WW2, and in 1945 its directors stated that the company had 'ceased to exist'. Miraculously, the tooling for the humble 170 saloon had escaped, and this little car went back

# Mercedes 300SL

into production, easing Germany's need for basic transport. In 1951, Mercedes brought out the big 300 saloon that became synonymous with chancellor Adenauer's government.

Mercedes wanted to go racing, but had nothing in the way of blueprints on which to base a sports car except the staid 300, the tall, heavy engine of which was not what was wanted in a cutting-edge competition vehicle. Tipping the engine over to 40° dealt with the height, and they built the rest of the car super-light to compensate for the engine's bulk: the answer was a space frame made of dozens of small diameter tubes.

The new car was a sensation, winning both Le Mans and the Carrera Panamericana in 1952. It was called the 300SL, but it was only a racing car – and that's the way it would have stayed if it hadn't been for New York car importer Max Hoffmann, who saw the potential of the 300SL as a road car in the US. The factory wasn't really interested until Hoffmann made a firm order for 1,000 cars.

In 1954, the 300SL became a road car. Where the racer had been aerodynamic but ugly, the road car was stunning. It kept the upward opening doors of the racer, and this led to its being universally called the 'Gullwing'.

It was the first road car with a fuel-injected engine, and with 195bhp it could top 150mph with a high ratio axle. However, this gem was not without its flaws: the suspension was taken from the 300 saloon, and at the back used a very old-fashioned swing axle design. This could cause a sudden breakaway, and the Gullwing killed a fair few drivers with more money than ability.

In 1957, the Gullwing gave way to the Roadster, which had large, one-piece headlights and regular doors. Most importantly, the rear suspension had been redesigned and the handling improved.

The 300SL created the SL tradition that lasts to this day, with the cars themselves more desirable now than at any point in their formidable history.

## Specifications

| | |
|---|---|
| Production dates | 1954-1957 (Gullwing); 1957-1963 (Roadster) |
| Manufactured units | 1,400 (Gullwing); 1,858 (Roadster) |
| Engine type | Straight 6 single overhead cam, fuel-injected |
| Engine size | 2,996cc |
| Maximum power | 195bhp (Gullwing); 215bhp (Roadster) |
| Transmission | 4-speed |
| Top speed | 125mph-150mph, dependent on final drive ratio |
| 0-60 mph time | 7-9 seconds, dependent on final drive ratio |
| Country of origin | Germany |

*Values for the Gullwing are higher than for the*
*Roadster, due to its overt racing heritage. In fact*
*the Roadster is better to drive, just as fast, and you*
*don't have to lift out the windows to keep cool!*

*Spaceship or goddess; to many the DS was both*

Citroen had long been known for adventurous and innovative engineering. The Light 15 of 1934, also known as the 'Traction Avant', pioneered mass-produced front-wheel drive and unitary construction and, when the DS19 landed in an unsuspecting world on Octber 5th, 1955, it was by far the most advanced car in the world.

The DS and cheaper ID (sounding like the French for 'goddess' and 'idea', respectively)

# Citroen DS

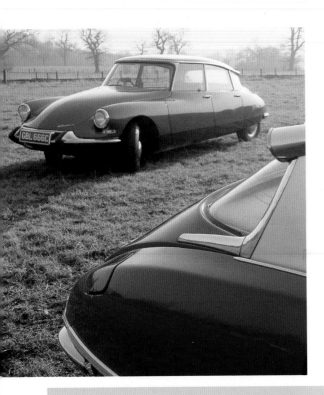

shared a rather old-fashioned engine, and had the engine behind the gearbox as had been seen in the Traction Avant, but everything else was new. Styling, by Faliminio Bertoni, and was like nothing seen before or since: the rear wheels were set so far back that the passenger space was enormous, while front-wheel drive allowed the floor to be flat. The rear indicators in the roof gutter looked like rockets, and the smooth bonnet and lack of a radiator grill were revolutionary. The interior was equally futuristic, with a single-spoked steering wheel that shocked the unprepared.

The car's life blood was its high-pressure hydraulic system. There were no steel springs and the suspension gave an unworldly soft ride, plus there was also the ability to adjust the ride height, although the DS's party trick was its ability to

drive on three wheels (which allowed drivers to change a wheel without a jack). The brake pedal was a button, the sensitivity of which caught out every novice driver first time, while the power steering utilised hydraulics, and some models even had hydraulic gear and clutch engagement (although the simpler ID boasted only the suspension and braking systems).

On paper, the DS did not appear especially fast, but its handling ability, combined with a talent for keeping its passengers cosseted during spirited driving, made it a formidable A-to-B machine.

As time went by, its designers came up with increases in power and sophistication, such as swivelling head lights. Later models were designated the DS20, DS21 and DS23. The Pallas, meanwhile, was a luxury model, the Safari was a cavernous estate, and there was even a coupé and a convertible by Chapron, both highly prized collectors' items with prices to match.

On the DS's 50th anniversary, Paris ground to a halt as thousands of DSs came to celebrate their birthday. There are few objects the French are more proud of than the DS, and enthusiasts everywhere display a loyalty verging on obsession.

### Specifications

| | |
|---|---|
| Production dates | 1955-1975 |
| Manufactured units | 1,456,115 |
| Engine type | 4-cylinder pushrod OHV |
| Engine size | 1,911cc; 1,985cc; 2,175cc; 2,347cc |
| Maximum power | 109bhp (DS21) |
| Transmission | 4-manual and semi-automatic, front-wheel drive |
| Top speed | 106mph (DS21) |
| 0-60 mph time | 14.8 seconds (DS21) |
| Country of origin | France |

*Though most DSs provided everyday transport for the French middle classes, the convertible by Chapron was something rare and special. Today these wear a price tag that is truly exclusive*

*For the T-Bird, first was best, as the purity of the two-seater cars was never fully recaptured*

It was Chevrolet that made the Thunderbird happen. In 1953, it brought out the Corvette, and GM certainly weren't going to have anything that Ford didn't have. Ford wanted a more practical vehicle than the 'Vette, so, rather than calling the T-Bird a sports car, it termed its new creation a 'personal' car.

The T-Bird fused low-slung elegance with a thoroughly Ford look. It was not the out-and-out

# '55-'57 Ford Thunderbird

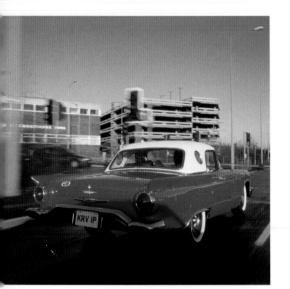

sports car that the early Corvette had tried and failed to be. It sat on the same 102in wheelbase, but there were proper wind-up windows, a power top and a lift-off hard top. Under the hood was a beefy 193bhp Mercury V8, while the 'Vette struggled with flappy side screens and a limp six pot. Under that gorgeous skin it might have run on standard Ford parts from lesser models in the range, but who cared?

On release in 1955 it was priced at an irresistible $3,000, and as a result managed to outsell the Corvette that year by an incredible 24 to one.

Detroit restyled its models every season in the 1950s, but the runaway success of the T-Bird meant that it was too good to change. For 1956 it received a 'continental' spare wheel on the back, a little more power and softer suspension. It also

got the no-cost option of distinctive portholes in the hard top. Remember the mystery girl's white T-Bird in 'American Graffiti'?

For 1957 there was a light makeover, with a different bumper and grill, and a longer rear deck for more trunk space. Elegance was undiminished, and you could now get up to 285bhp if you ticked the right boxes. They even went racing with a 340bhp supercharged version – only 208 were built, and success was limited.

Ford wanted greater sales, and for 1958 the T-Bird became a four seater. The new car was so ugly that even its mother couldn't have loved it, but the American public did, and it sold twice as well as the two-seater cars had.

The T-Bird would never be a two-seater again, but the 1961 to 1963 cars regained a beauty and simplicity of line, and would later feature in the film 'Thelma and Louise'.

The 1964 model held on to some of its predecessors' looks, but from there on it was downhill all the way, with the T-Bird becoming a car for men wearing white shoes and plaid slacks.

## Specifications

| | |
|---|---|
| Production dates | 1955-1957 |
| Manufactured units | 53,166 |
| Engine type | V8 pushrod OHV |
| Engine size | 4,785cc; 5,112cc |
| Maximum power | 193bhp-285bhp |
| Transmission | 3-speed manual with optional overdrive, or 3-speed automatic |
| Top speed | 105mph-125mph |
| 0-60 mph time | 11.5-7.0 seconds |
| Country of origin | USA |

*the runaway success of the*
*Bird meant that it was*
*o good to change*

*Few cars have been as right as the '55 Chevy with its new V8. Except perhaps the '57*

The '54 Chevy was upright, old fashioned and had a dull six under the hood. The all-new '55 Chevy, on the other hand, could not have been more different.

GM styling chief Harley Earl instructed his staff to 'go all the way, then back off'. The result was three years of Chevys that are affectionately known as the 'Tri Chevys', and remain revered the world over to this day.

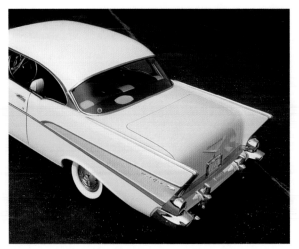

# '55, '56, '57 Chevrolets

For 1956, there was a gentle restyle, and the pillarless two-door car was joined by a 'hard top' four-door pillarless sedan. The restyle was successful, but today the '56 is less sought after than its '55 and '57 cousins.

There was a new lighter chassis frame underneath, but it was the clean, perfectly proportioned looks that got noticed. So did the engine: 1955 saw the birth of the 'Small Block' V8, super-modern in design and built for high revs and low weight.

There were two- and four-door cars, a four-door station wagon, a convertible, and three ranges – the One-Ten, Two-Ten, and the desirable Bel Air. Then there was the Nomad: a station wagon styling exercise on the Corvette was so well received at shows that the design was rapidly adapted for the '55 model. The two-door wagon was stunning: it cost more than the convertible and sold slowly, but Tri Chevy Nomads remain a collector's dream.

1955 was a boom year, and Chevrolet sold 1.7 million cars, taking a full 44% of the lower-priced market.

Perhaps they saved the best till last. Designer Carl Renner said they had tried to make the car, 'look like a little Cadillac'. It worked, and with tail fins and bumper bullets in the grill it was hard to believe that this was still the same basic hull as in the '55. It might have lost the unadorned simplicity of the '55, but it didn't matter.

In 1957, Chevy gave the option of fuel injection – a first on an American car, and not so far behind Mercedes Benz with the 300SL. It made 283bhp and blasted the '57 to 60 in eight seconds, but cost a whopping $500, so only 1,503 'Fuelies' got built.

No cars better epitomise the decade than the Tri Chevys. All of them are true classics, but if you find yourself a Nomad, convertible or a Fuelie, better talk to you bank manager first, as they tend to go for truly phenomenal prices.

## Specifications

| | |
|---|---|
| Production dates | 1955, 1956, 1957 |
| Manufactured units | 1,703,993 ('55); 1,563,729 ('56) 1,499,658 ('57) |
| Engine type | Straight 6 and V8 OHV |
| Engine size | 3,850cc (straight 6); 4,342cc/4,637cc (V8) |
| Maximum power | 162bhp-283bhp (V8) |
| Transmission | 3-speed manual with optional overdrive, or 2-speed automatic |
| Top speed | 90mph-120mph (V8) |
| 0-60 mph time | 11.4-8.0 seconds (V8) |
| Country of origin | USA |

*The '57 was the last of the "Tri Chevys"*
*and in two-door Bel Air hardtop form,*
*as here, it has a perfection of line*
*that you just can't knock*

*The DB Astons were the epitome of the post-war sports car, with exceptional lines and success on the track*

Aston Martin got its name from the English village of Aston Clinton, where Lionel Martin had competed in hill climbs. The first Aston Martin appeared in 1914, and in 1921 came racing success at the Brooklands track. The company built small-engined, hand-made sports cars that were very special, but very expensive. It first went bust in 1924, and from then on was always on a shaky financial footing.

# Aston Martin DB4/DB5

In 1947, the company was bought by tractor magnate David Brown. A four-cylinder engine had been designed, but Brown wanted more. He had also purchased Lagonda, and with it came a twin overhead cam six-cylinder unit, which had been designed by the great W.O Bentley, and was used to power his Astons.

The DB2 of 1949 was a sleek coupé along the lines of Ferraris at the time. Rather confusingly, it developed to become the DB2/4, DB2/4 Mk II, and the DB Mk III. The DB3 was a sports racing car, as were the DB3S and the DBR 1, which won both Le Mans and the World Sports Car Championship for David Brown in 1959.

The DB4 in 1958 was all new, including its engine, designed by Polish engineer Tadek

Marek. It was another twin-cam six, but larger at 3,670cc. It was claimed to make 240bhp, and to give the DB4 a top speed of 140mph, both claims that may have been a little enthusiastic.

The styling was svelte and lithe, and the unique bodywork was handmade using the 'superleggera', or 'super light', technique of Carrozzeria Touring of Milan.

In 1962 there came a convertible. There was a faster Vantage version, and a very fast short wheelbase DB4 GT. Then there were 19 GTs with beautiful bodies built by Zagato in Italy.

In 1963 the DB4 became the DB5. It used the faired-in lights of the GT, but looked little different to the DB4. The engine was enlarged to 3,995cc and there was 282bhp available. The DB6 in 1965 was a heavier, less elegant motor car.

The DB5 shot to worldwide fame when Sean Connery's James Bond drove one in 'Goldfinger'. The Corgi toy sold in millions to small boys, and although they're all grown up, for most of them the DB5 remains as unattainable as ever.

## Specifications

| | |
|---|---|
| Production dates | 1958-1963 (DB4); 1963-1965 (DB5) |
| Manufactured units | 1,110 (DB4); 1,021 (DB5) |
| Engine type | Twin-cam 6-cylinder |
| Engine size | 3,670cc (DB4); 3,995cc (DB5) |
| Maximum power | 240bhp (DB4); 285bhp (DB5); 315bph (DB4 Zagato) |
| Transmission | 4-speed sychromesh |
| Top speed | 140mph+ |
| 0-60 mph time | 8.1 seconds |
| Country of origin | UK |

*The Aston Martin DB4 sets the gold standard for classics. Beautiful, fast, rare and, above all, utterly desirable*

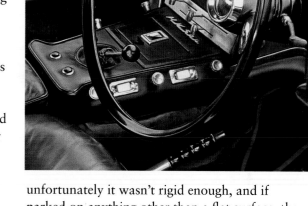

In the early 1950s, the Facel company of wealthy industrialist Jean Daninos was making everything from kitchen sinks to jet engine parts. Then it started making bodies for auto makers such as Simca, Panhard and Ford. The French Ford Comete of 1952 was a pretty coupé, but Daninos wanted to build his own car.

In 1954 he presented the Facel Vega FVS. Powered by one of the best engines of the day, the Chrysler

*The exotic HK500 never quite fitted in, but remains one of the most romantic cars ever made*

# Facel Vega HK500

'Hemi' V8, it was fast and very beautiful. Its styling was truly 'transatlantic', with an unmistakable American influence filtered through European sensibilities, while the wrap-around windscreen and forward lean gave it a unique look. The Facel was the first of several British and Italian–American hybrids, but none achieved the perfect fusion of styles seen in the Facel.

The engineering was straightforward and heavy, following US practice with a hefty tubular chassis and solid rear axle – and with only drum brakes to slow it down, it was arguably better at speeding up than stopping!

A stretched four-door FVS called the Excellence arrived in 1958. With pillarless construction and suicide rear doors it looked incredible, but

unfortunately it wasn't rigid enough, and if parked on anything other than a flat surface, the doors would refuse to open.

In 1959 the FVS became the HK500, with an even bigger 5,907cc Chrysler V8, while later cars had a 6,286cc engine with up to 390bhp! Unfortunately, the chassis wasn't really up to it, the steering said to be 'vega' than most. The styling was perfected, and the cars were equally spectacular on the inside. The aircraft style wrap-around dashboard appeared to be in heavily figured burr walnut, but in fact it was steel, painted by a talented *tromp l'oeil* artist.

Everything about the HK500 is romantic – even the legends that surround it. Nobel Prize-winning author and philosopher Albert Camus died in one during an accident near Paris. His friend and agent, who was driving, also perished.

In 1962 came the Facel II, with a totally different look. The big V8 cars were always slow sellers, but it was Daninos' ill-fated venture building his own small sports-car engine that eventually sank the company.

The HK500 isn't really a very good car, but with charisma and presence in spades, who cares?

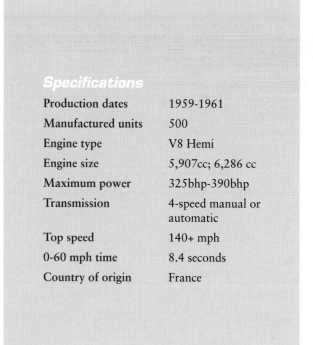

| Specifications | |
|---|---|
| Production dates | 1959-1961 |
| Manufactured units | 500 |
| Engine type | V8 Hemi |
| Engine size | 5,907cc; 6,286 cc |
| Maximum power | 325bhp-390bhp |
| Transmission | 4-speed manual or automatic |
| Top speed | 140+ mph |
| 0-60 mph time | 8.4 seconds |
| Country of origin | France |

*Beloved of both bank managers and bank robbers, the Mk II is still the greatest Jaguar saloon*

William Lyons and William Walmsley set up their Swallow Sidecars business as very young men in 1922. By 1927, they had progressed to building bodies on Austin Seven chassis. They looked extravagant but were keenly priced, and sold well. In 1931 came their first proper car: the SS. In 1935, a new six-cylinder saloon and sports car were launched, both called the SS Jaguar. The cars looked to be in the same class as Bentleys, but at a quarter of the price.

# Jaguar Mk II

After the Second World War, the SS name could no longer be used due to its unpleasant connotations of Nazi stormtroopers.

There was soon a new Jaguar engine on the block. This was the legendary twin overhead cam, six-cylinder XK unit. It powered both the XK sports cars and the Mk VII, VIII and IX saloons. These were big cars, but the XK engine endowed them with remarkable performance.

Something sportier was needed, and in 1955 the much smaller Mk I was released. With the same 3.4-litre engine as its big brother, it was considerably quicker. It was an instant hit, but when Jaguar developed it into the Mk II in 1959, it created its most famous saloon ever.

There was a wider rear track, and the glass house was given much lighter styling. Under the bonnet you could have the 2.4 or 3.4 from the

Mk I, but there was now a 3.8. This endowed the Mk II with quite extraordinary performance, and 125mph could be rung out of it on Britain's unrestricted motorways. There were new disc brakes all round, as pioneered by Jaguar on its competition cars. It handled well, but by modern standards the gearbox and steering were heavy and hard work. Inside was as much leather and wood as you would find in a Rolls Royce, and all this for the bargain price of £1,444 including tax, for the 2.4.

The Mk II dominated the new production saloon racing, but there were other, less salubrious characters who also appreciated its performance. The Mk II became infamous as the bank robber's get away car of choice, and no self-respecting 1960s cop drama was complete without a tyre-smoking Mk II.

Today, the Mk II is both archetypally British and a quintessential icon of the 1960s – as attractive a package now as it ever was.

## Specifications

| | |
|---|---|
| Production dates | 1959-1967 |
| Manufactured units | 83,976 |
| Engine type | Twin overhead cam 6-cylinder |
| Engine size | 2,483cc; 3,442cc; 3,781cc |
| Maximum power | 120bhp; 210bhp; 220bhp |
| Transmission | 4-speed with optional overdrive |
| Top speed | 125mph (3.8) |
| 0-60 mph time | 8.5 seconds (3.8) |
| Country of origin | UK |

The Mk II was formidable on the track. Seen here cresting Paddock Hill and braking for Druids corner at Brands Hatch, the "BUY 12" registration gives the white car away as a 'Coombes' Jaguar, from John Coombes garage in Guildford

*If ever a car proved that you don't have to go fast to have fun, it was the 'Frogeye'*

Donald Healey had worked for various British car makers before and during WW2, and in 1945 he was quick to acquire a factory in Warwick, England.

His first cars were powered by Riley engines, and as coupés, convertibles, and sports cars around 600 units were sold. A collaboration with Nash in America created the equally successful Nash-Healey, which sold only in the US.

# Austin-Healey Sprite

In the early 1950s, boss of BMC Sir Leonard Lord, which included both Austin and Morris, was on the lookout for a sports-car design. He liked what Healey showed him and the Healey 100 was the result. Meanwhile, Healey was happy because he didn't even have to build the cars!

The 100 gained a six-cylinder engine, becoming the 100/6 and later the 3000. In the mid-1950s there was a gap in the market for a small, no-frills sports car, and Healey was asked to develop one: the Austin-Healey Sprite of 1958.

The designer responsible for the big Healey's lovely lines had departed, and the Sprite ended up with rather 'individual' styling. The headlights popping out of the bonnet gave rise to its

enduring nickname of the 'Frogeye', but the quirky looks only added to the little car's charm.

Charm it had aplenty, and although its top speed was only 83mph, it was a hoot to drive. The little 948cc A-Series engine from the Austin A35 saloon had a lively and eager character quite at odds with its humble specification. The front suspension also came from the little Austin, but 1/4 elliptic rear springs located the axle much better. It was light, nimble, and had perfect balance – all thanks to its simplicity. There were no locks, no boot, no proper windows, and you had to reach inside to open a door.

A more conventional restyle came in 1961, and the Sprite was joined by the near-identical MG Midget. Engines got bigger and weight increased. The last Sprite was made in 1971, but the Midget soldiered on until 1980, by which time it was a rather overweight shadow of the first Sprite.

The Frogeye was the original cheeky little sports car, and still engenders enormous affection in its many devotees.

## Specifications

| | |
|---|---|
| Production dates | 1959-1961 |
| Manufactured units | 48,987 |
| Engine type | 4-cylinder pushrod OHV |
| Engine size | 948cc |
| Maximum power | 43bhp |
| Transmission | 4-speed, synchromesh on top 3 gears |
| Top speed | 83mph |
| 0-60 mph time | 18 seconds |
| Country of origin | UK |

*In the 1950s, the American dream had come true, and the '59 was perhaps its ultimate manifestation*

Has there ever been a car so famed for just one feature? With the '59 Caddies it was all about those fins. For 1960 they'd been trimmed back, and by 1965 fins were just a memory for the American auto industry.

It was all their fault in the first place. Harley Earl, or 'Misterearl', as he was always referred to, had pretty much come up with the idea of car styling. At General Motors in 1925 he introduced the concept of annual model changes and – although he wouldn't have put it this way – designed obsolescence. When GM formed its Art and Colour section in 1927, Earl was in charge. It started with 50 people, but was to grow to 1,400.

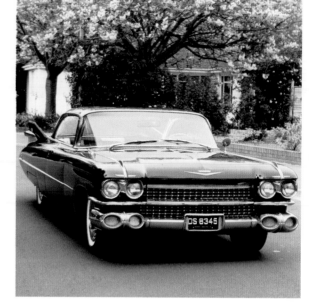

# Cadillac

Making cars look good, and making them different every year, made them sell. The rest of Detroit had to play catch up.

Come the end of WW2, the US was set to enter its golden decade. It was a unique time of economic boom, confidence, and cultural innocence, but the Bay of Pigs and Kennedy's assassination brought it all to an end.

This was the jet age, the TV age, the space age, and the greatest time there had ever been to be an American. Americans wanted their cars to reflect their dreams, and Misterearl obliged.

Back in 1941, Earl had seen the still secret P38 Lightning fighter plane. He took the beautiful tail fin shape and applied it to his '48 Cadillacs.

Throughout the 1950s, US styling grew more outrageous, as did the prominence of the fins. There were some biggies on Chryslers and Plymouths, but the '59 Caddie's beat them all. With twin bullet lights mounted half way up, looking like small rockets, style had completely triumphed over function.

The '59 wasn't even a very good car, but no-one noticed. It had a V8 under the hood, like any other Cadillac, but no-one asked any questions. Sure, the front end suffered from vibration and it handled badly. So what?

The '59 is the ultimate icon of rock 'n' roll Americana: a reminder of the good times when the good times were never going to end. Another way to see it might be as an old-fashioned, inefficient relic, heaving its last gasp while dressed up in preposterous fancy dress. Vietnam was just around the corner.

## Specifications

| | |
|---|---|
| Production dates | 1959 |
| Manufactured units | 142,272 |
| Engine type | V8 OHV |
| Engine size | 6,390cc |
| Maximum power | 325/345bhp |
| Transmission | Hydra-Matic auto |
| Top speed | 120mph |
| 0-60 mph time | 11.5 |
| Country of origin | USA |

*The '59 is the ultimate icon of
rock 'n' roll Americana*

94

*The Mini put more new ideas into 10ft than had ever been seen in one car before*

Alex Issigonis was a genuine genius. During the fuel crisis of 1956, he put his extraordinary mind to creating a new sort of small car – and no small car has been packaged as well as the Mini. His first big idea was to turn the engine across the car. Most cars have transverse engines these days, but the Mini was the first. Then he put the gearbox under the engine, in its sump. This meant them sharing their oil, but developments in lubrication meant this wasn't a problem.

# Mini

The suspension used rubber for springs, which saved space again. Issigonis didn't like wasting space on a boot that was seldom used, so the lid to the tiny boot opened downwards, and larger loads could be carried with the boot open. This left more room for passengers, and the Mini was something of a Tardis. To make manufacture cheaper, the body's seams were turned outwards, welded together and covered with trim.

And all this innovation came in a 10ft package. Issigonis' previous small car, the Morris Minor, had been a full 28in longer!

The car was so light that, on its release in 1959, the engine size was reduced from 950cc to 850cc, because it was too fast! It was the first classless car, driven by Peter Sellers and his cleaning lady alike. It was immediately super trendy and stayed that way, epitomising Cool Britannia and the swinging '60s.

The Mini was a blast to drive, and pretty soon there were faster Cooper and Cooper S versions available. They were unbeatable on the track or rally stage, and giant killing became routine, including a triple on the Monte Carlo Rally. Anyone who has ever driven a Cooper S will know that it's impossible to drive one slowly!

The Mini's place in every British heart was sealed when three Mini Coopers starred in 'The Italian Job' in 1969, which featured Michael Caine and a seemingly endless supply of unforgettable lines.

The Mini came as a van, a pickup, and a Traveller estate with wood trim. There were luxury Riley Elf and Wolseley Hornet versions, and later the Clubman and 1,275GT. No other car ever approached its dimensions and still carried four in reasonable comfort. Its unique status meant it looked as though it would last forever, but time was finally called on October 4th 2000, when the last Mini rolled off the production line.

### Specifications

| | |
|---|---|
| Production dates | 1959-2000 |
| Manufactured units | 5,387,862 |
| Engine type | 4-cylinder transverse |
| Engine size | 848cc-1,275cc |
| Maximum power | 34bhp-76bhp |
| Transmission | 4-speed in sump |
| Top speed | 72mph-96mph |
| 0-60 mph time | 29.7-10.5 seconds |
| Country of origin | UK |

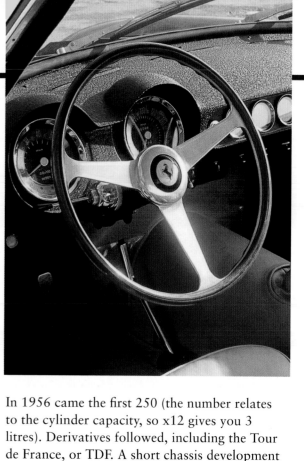

*No other car has combined everyday roadability and weekend track talent like the SWB*

In 1928, Enzo Ferrari founded Scuderia Ferrari, a racing team competing in the fabulous Alfa Romeo racing cars of the time. He built a couple of cars in 1940, but the Ferrari name didn't appear on a car until after WW2.

Throughout the 1950s, 'Il Commendatore', as Enzo was known, was only really interested in racing – his road cars were simply a way to finance the competition programme.

# Ferrari 250GT SWB

The first Ferrari appeared in 1946 with a 2.0-litre V12 engine designed by the great Gioacchino Columbo, and was winning races by 1947. The first road cars came a year later, powered by versions of the V12. The trouble was that Enzo was giving his attention to winning Grand Prix, something his team were pretty good at. They lifted the World Championship in 1952, 1953, and 1958, with further titles in 1961 and 1964. They also won Le Mans in 1949, 1954, 1958, and 1960 straight through to 1965.

The 1950s road cars were beautiful, fast, and certainly exclusive. But they were also under-developed and often too close to competition models to be practical. Many were raced in sports-car events, but unless you had a works car you were unlikely to win.

In 1956 came the first 250 (the number relates to the cylinder capacity, so x12 gives you 3 litres). Derivatives followed, including the Tour de France, or TDF. A short chassis development appeared in 1960, and the 250GT Short Wheel Base Berlinetta was born. Bodywork was styled by Pininfarina and built by Scaglietti. You could have it in steel or aluminium, and no two cars were exactly the same. In spite of this, it was the first real series-produced Ferrari.

Production-car racing was very popular, and the 250SWB was the car to drive if you wanted to win. What was unique about the SWB was that it really could be driven to the shops, then driven to the track, raced, and driven home again. You wouldn't have wanted to go shopping in a TDF, and the 250GTO that followed the SWB was a pure racing car with little pretence of being domesticated, but otherwise the principles of the cars remained the same.

The GTO may be more famous, but the SWB is still the greatest dual-purpose car ever built.

## Specifications

| | |
|---|---|
| Production dates | 1960-1962 |
| Manufactured units | 165 |
| Engine type | 60-degree V12 |
| Engine size | 2,953cc |
| Maximum power | 220bhp-280bhp |
| Transmission | 4-speed synchromesh |
| Top speed | 145mph-155mph |
| 0-60 mph time | 6.3 seconds |
| Country of origin | Italy |

*The GTO may be more famous, but the SWB is still the greatest dual-purpose car ever built*

*The 180 made Mercedes
a major manufacturer.
But is it a classic...?*

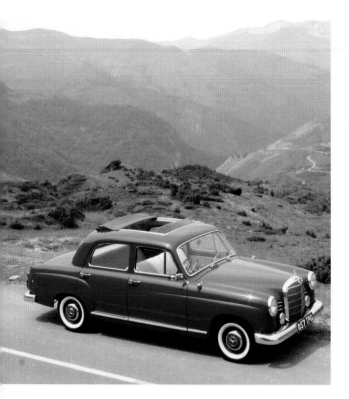

After WW2 Daimler Benz started building a small pre-war model, and it proved to be its salvation. This model had a clever cruciform separate chassis, and even the company's new 300 limousine shared this design. Something more modern was needed, and it would have to embrace the new unitary body construction techniques.

In 1953 came the 180. It was simply styled, perhaps even a little dumpy. The engine and front

# Mercedes Benz 180

suspension was carried on a separate subframe – a little like a pontoon bridge – which led to this shape of Mercedes always being referred to as the 'Pontoon'. Volvo claims to have pioneered crumple zones but, in fact, the 180 was the first car to incorporate the concept.

Engines were the slow, wheezy, diesel, and side-valve petrol units from the old 170. Not until 1957 did the 180 get a detuned version of the overhead cam engine from the 190SL, and decent performance.

The model shown here (the author's car) has been to Spain twice, France several times, and has visited Italy, Sicily, Belgium, Holland, Luxembourg, Switzerland, and Wales. On these journeys it cruised at 75mph, even though the top speed is only 84mph. There have been one or two problems, but nothing that stopped it from getting home. Just to prove that using an old car doesn't do it any harm, it has also won its class in the Mercedes Benz Club national concours. It might have a few stone chips, but it wears them with pride.

But is it a classic? The public's reaction speaks for itself – in Italy, the car was greeted with cries of, 'Bella, bella' and in south London West Indian guys shout, 'Cool car man'...

## Specifications

| | |
|---|---|
| Production dates | 1953-1962; 1959-1961 (189b) |
| Manufactured units | 271,217 (all types) |
| Engine type | 4-cylinder petrol, OHC (180b) |
| Engine size | 1,897cc (180b) |
| Maximum power | 68bhp (180b) |
| Transmission | 4-speed synchromesh, column change |
| Top speed | 84mph |
| 0-60 mph time | 18 seconds |
| Country of origin | Germany |

*America loved it so much that they bought most of them. No export has done more for Britain's image than the E-Type Jag*

Few cars have caused a storm like the one at the unveiling of the E-Type in 1961. The XK120 of 1948 had been cutting edge, but by now it had developed into the XK150 and was fairly antiquated. With a heavy separate chassis it was tall and old-fashioned. Its replacement could not have been more different.

Jaguar had been extremely successful in sports-car racing during the 1950s, with Le Mans victories

# Jaguar E-Type

in 1951, 1953, and 1955 through to 1957. First there had been the C-Type, with the brand new technology of disc brakes. Then came the D-Type with its aerodynamic form and unitary chassis. All the lessons learnt at the La Sarthe track were used in the design of the E-Type.

There were Dunlop disc brakes all round, and the body was of unitary, or monocoque, construction. This allowed it to be low, and it's hard to think of a car that looks lower than the E-Type. It plainly owed much to the lines of the D-Type, but that was a racing car and didn't have to sell. The E-Type shared the same small oval grill and faired-in lights, but it was styled to please – and please it did. The roadster and the fixed-head coupé vied to be the most beautiful car in the world.

A press car was tested to 150.4mph. Though it may have had a little extra care in its preparation, customers' cars could get very close to this magic number. The same car reached 60 in 6.9 seconds.

It wasn't just fast and beautiful. With sophisticated independent rear suspension it handled well and rode like no sports car before it. This was a car in which to cross continents.

The E-Type had one more trump card up its sleeve – it was cheap. Jags had always been good value, and combined with great performance, this had created a slightly unwelcome image. A derogatory term for the middle classes was 'the Jag and gin brigade'. All this was forgotten with the E-Type – it was just too good to knock.

Its unique combination of qualities mean the E-Type will never go out of fashion, yet even now it's remarkable value next to an Aston or Ferrari.

## Specifications

| | |
|---|---|
| Production dates | 1961-1973 (all types) |
| Manufactured units | 72,584 (all types) |
| Engine type | 6-cylinder twin overhead cam |
| Engine size | 3,781cc (pre-1964) |
| Maximum power | 265bhp |
| Transmission | 4-speed sychromesh |
| Top speed | 150mph |
| 0-60 mph time | 7.1 seconds |
| Country of origin | UK |

*With world-beating performance
and looks to die for, it's hard
to believe that the E-type
was also cheap*

*The MGB was a sports car for every man. The MGB GT was a sports car for every man and his dog*

Ever since the end of WW2, MG seem to have been selling old-fashioned cars to old-fashioned people. With the release of the MGB in 1962, that was to change – at least for a while.

The MGA had been a direct development of the T series cars, with their pre-war roots. In spite of this, it was too modern for many British sports-car enthusiasts – who would have been shocked by its replacement, the thoroughly modern B.

# MGB

The B was of monocoque construction. This wasn't exactly ground breaking, but the Austin-Healey and Triumph opposition were still built on separate chassis. The mechanical bits came from the rather mundane Austin and Morris saloons. The B series engine was tuned to 95bhp and that meant 100mph. It was enough to make the B an instant bestseller.

In 1965 came a coupé version with small back seats. The clever bit was an opening rear hatch, considerably pre-dating the hatchback boom. The MGB GT's back seats weren't very useful, but there was plenty of room for the dog and the shopping. Practicality meant excellent sales.

By the 1970s, the B was long in the tooth, and MG were back to selling simple outdated cars to those who could not embrace modernity. In

1974, the disastrous decision was made to fit all MGBs with the US spec 5mph impact bumpers. The MGB became a bit of a joke – in fact, with hindsight, the rubber bumper cars drive almost identically to earlier cars, but they do look awful.

Management indifference and incompetence meant that no successor to the B was developed, and, with complete inevitability, the MG factory closed in 1980.

There had been interesting variations on the MGB theme, but none were properly developed or marketed. The MGC of 1967 was powered by a modernised version of the 3.0-litre Healey's engine. Unfortunately, it was underpowered, and the great weight of the engine ruined the B's tidy handling. The MGB GT V8 of 1973 was much better. The lightweight Rover V8 meant 125mph and 0 to 60 in just 8 seconds, but only 2,591 of these misunderstood coupés were made.

It's no road burner, but as a sports car to live with, the B still takes some beating.

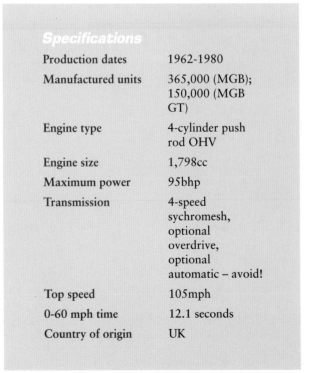

## Specifications

| | |
|---|---|
| Production dates | 1962-1980 |
| Manufactured units | 365,000 (MGB); 150,000 (MGB GT) |
| Engine type | 4-cylinder push rod OHV |
| Engine size | 1,798cc |
| Maximum power | 95bhp |
| Transmission | 4-speed sychromesh, optional overdrive, optional automatic – avoid! |
| Top speed | 105mph |
| 0-60 mph time | 12.1 seconds |
| Country of origin | UK |

*With excellent performance and a V8 rumble, the MGB GT V8 was the best of all the Bs. It was never built as a roadster, and poor management prevented it from achieving its potential*

*Record sales plus record victories made the Mk I 'Tina an all-time classic*

In the early 1960s, the choice of mid-range cars made in Britain was grim. Ford's Consul Classic was plain ugly, and sales were slow, but the Cortina of 1962 was as right as the Classic was wrong.

The name came from the 1956 Winter Olympics venue, Cortina di Ampezzo, in the Italian Dolomites. It was initially to be called 'Caprino', but this was shelved when it became apparent that in Italian this meant 'goat dung'!

# Ford Cortina

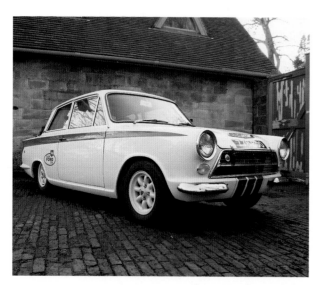

There was nothing revolutionary about the car, as all of its mechanical parts came from other Fords, but the sum of its parts was greater, and the crisp-looking 'Tina was just what the British family man wanted – and at £639, he could afford it.

There soon came a 1500 to add to the 1200, with the option of two or four doors, or an estate. The product planners knew what people wanted, and in 1963 came the GT. This was the first sporty British Ford, and was the start of a dynasty that continues to this day. With 78bhp, it was capable of reaching 90mph, and with lower suspension and wider wheels it was every boy racer's dream – or it would have been, if the Lotus Cortina hadn't come along.

'Race on Sunday, sell on Monday', was an ethos never better expressed than in the Lotus Cortina.

Colin Chapman's company developed a twin-cam version of Ford's 1500 engine for its Elan, and this was to power the new car. There was much modified running gear, including a rear suspension that often fell apart, but such things were easily overlooked: after all, the car was a sensation on the track. Driven by masters such as world champion Jim Clark, it seemed to have at least one wheel off the ground on every corner. All but unbeatable then, it remains so today in historic saloon-car racing. The Lotus cost twice the price of a basic 1200 when new, but you'd have to pay a lot more for one now.

In 1966 came the Mk II Cortina, and the final Mk V 'Tina finally bowed out in 1982, being replaced by the Sierra.

The Cortina was the UK's best-selling car for two decades, and continues to occupy a unique place in British popular culture.

## Specifications

| | |
|---|---|
| Production dates | 1962-1966 |
| Manufactured units | 1,013,391 |
| Engine type | 4-cylinder, twin cam (Lotus) |
| Engine size | 1,198cc; 1,498cc; 1,558cc (Lotus) |
| Maximum power | 50bhp (1200); 61.5bhp (1500); 78bhp (GT); 105bhp (Lotus) |
| Transmission | 4-speed manual with automatic option |
| Top speed | 78mph-107mph |
| 0-60 mph time | 8 seconds (Lotus) |
| Country of origin | UK |

*The Lotus Cortina was a giant killer in its day, its glory on the track reflected in the imagination of every salesman who drove a 1200 Deluxe*

*For some, too much is never enough.*
*The Cobra is the car for them*

AC (which stands for Autocarriers), had been building cars in Thames Ditton, south of London, since 1904. After WW2, they resumed production by putting the six-cylinder engine they had been making since 1921 into a rather ungainly saloon. Things improved when they adopted a design by John Tojeiro, based rather closely on the contemporary Ferrari Barcetta. This was the AC Ace of 1954, and as well as fitting their own engine, AC also used Bristol and Ford units later

# AC Cobra

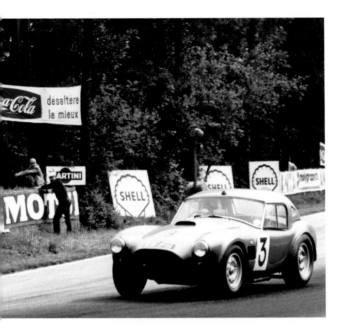

on. The Ace, particularly with Bristol power, was quick, good looking, and handled a treat.

In 1961, Bristol stopped making their engine, preferring to utilise the easy power of an American V8, and AC soon followed suit.

Texan racing driver Carroll Shelby fitted a Ford V8 to an Ace, and the rest, as they say, is history. Starting with a 4.2-litre, it was soon the 4.7, or 289 cubic inch, that was used. The old chassis coped manfully with twice the power it was designed for.

Even the 350bhp that the 289 could be persuaded to push out wasn't enough, and Shelby set about squeezing in the 7.0-litre 427 big block. This time, some big changes were needed to give the chassis a fighting chance. The antiquated transverse leaf springs were gone in favour of wishbones and coils. The chassis tubes were also enlarged.

The 289 was an animal, but the 427 was a monster. To accommodate much fatter rubber, the

wheel arches were widened, giving the appearance of a body builder's biceps. No car has ever looked tougher, or had more muscle to back it up. If the 425bhp of the standard 427 wasn't quite enough, you could order up a 485. 'Motor' magazine tested such a car, accelerating to 100mph in a phenomenal 10.1 seconds!

There was success on the track, as one might expect, and there were several beautiful Daytona coupés built just for racing.

No car has been as copied as the 427 Cobra, its brutish good looks making it irresistible to kit car builders. And yet, opinions divulge wildly. There are those who say that the Cobra's chassis could never really cope, making the handling twitchy and difficult. Amongst the acolytes there are also those who say it's the most overrated car in history. Unfortunately, few of us will ever have the chance to find out.

## Specifications

| | |
|---|---|
| Production dates | 1962-1969 |
| Manufactured units | 560 (289); 510 (427) |
| Engine type | V8 pushrod OHV |
| Engine size | 4,727cc (289); 6,997cc (427) |
| Maximum power | 270bhp-485bhp |
| Transmission | 4-speed manual |
| Top speed | 160mph |
| 0-60 mph time | 4.6 seconds (427) |
| Country of origin | UK, engine USA |

*If imitation really is the sincerest form of flattery, then the Cobra should be the greatest car of all time. Fibreglass kit car replicas have made the shape familiar, but it's still a fabulous-looking car*

*The Avanti was a heroic failure, but one that refused to just lie down and die*

Studebaker had been around for a long time – in fact, longer than any other auto maker, as the brothers Studebaker first built covered wagons back in 1852! Fifty years later, they started on cars – but only electric ones. They didn't get around to a petrol car until 1911.

# Studebaker Avanti

Like most independent car makers, they usually had a hard time. Poor management in the 1920s and 1930s, followed by the Depression, meant receivership in 1933 and the suicide of Studebaker's president. The vice president was a better businessman, and with help he nursed the company back to health.

In 1938, we saw the first alliance with the creator of the Coke bottle, brilliant industrial designer Raymond Loewy. He was to be involved in all of Studebaker's finest moments – and, as a result, 1939 was a record year.

Loewy Studios styled the whole post-war range, and they looked so good that 1950 was another record year. The cars were great, but fighting the Big Three was always going to be a losing battle.

In 1953, Loewy's legendary Starlight coupé was born, which became the Hawk. It was a fabulous car, but circumstances were against it, and 1956 saw the unfortunate end of the Loewy Studio contract with the company.

By the early 1960s, sales were in the doldrums. Loewy was invited back to create an exotic sports car and revitalise the old company's image, and the result was the Avanti, with styling more innovative than any US car since the Cord. Nothing looked like the Avanti, and although it had never been near a wind tunnel, the sloping front and high tail meant that it was exceptionally slippery. It was powered by the Studebaker 289 cubic inch V8. It gave 240bhp, but it was possible to order a supercharger providing 290bhp.

They took a modified car to Bonneville and broke a hatful of records, including running 170.78mph in the flying mile. Unfortunately, problems in making the Avanti's fibreglass body held up its release – deposits were withdrawn and people bought Corvettes. Only a small number were sold before the company moved from its famous South Bend Indiana factory to Ontario and by 1966 Studebaker was no more.

The Avanti was just too good to die, however, and was taken back into successful production as the Avanti II. The new company was run by enthusiasts, and although it has changed hands a few times, you can still buy a brand new Avanti today.

## Specifications

| | |
|---|---|
| Production dates | 1963-1964 |
| Manufactured units | 4,643 |
| Engine type | V8, optional supercharger |
| Engine size | 4,733cc |
| Maximum power | 240bhp-290bhp |
| Transmission | 3-speed |
| Top speed | 120mph |
| 0-60 mph time | 7.9 seconds |
| Country of origin | US |

*The Avanti's styling was more innovative than any US car since the Cord*

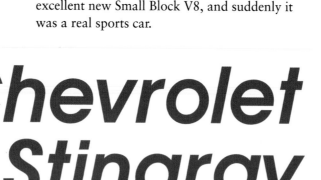

*The Stingray was a piece of automotive sculpture...with a V8!*

America's first sports car debuted in 1953. It was innovative in being the first mass-produced car with a fibreglass body. Unfortunately, the oily bits were less inspired, with the old-fashioned, 'Stovebolt' six engine, and two-speed powerglide transmission. It was slow, and so were sales. It nearly expired in 1955, but then along came the excellent new Small Block V8, and suddenly it was a real sports car.

# Chevrolet Corvette Stingray

For 1956 came a smart restyle, and in 1957 a four-speed gearbox and the option of fuel injection. Only 240 'Fuelies' were bought, but they could hit 60mph in 5.7 seconds. In 1958 there was another restyle, creating more weight, but more power too. In 1961, the rear end got a makeover, giving a subtle hint of what was to come.

The fabled Harley Earl had retired as head of GM's Art and Colour section, and Bill Mitchell's era had begun. The 1961 took its back end from a Mitchell styling exercise called the 'Stingray'.

For 1963 there was the first all-new Corvette since 1953 – the Stingray. Mitchell and his team had taken full advantage of the opportunities offered by fibreglass construction to sculpt a truly beautiful body. Design cues were all from the amazing Stingray concept car, while the roadster was now joined by an even more stunning coupé. This dramatic shape had the doors cut into the roof, and the 1963 models had a divided rear screen. These cars are highly sought after.

Under the plastic skin was a new chassis, and a first on a US production car – independent rear suspension. Engines were all 327 cubic inch V8s, with up to 360bhp available.

From the headlights hidden in its pointy nose, to its delicate rear quarter bumpers, it was a hit. Production doubled on the previous year, with around 20,000 cars sold.

Looks were too good to change, and there were only detailed differences year to year. Power went up and up, with a 427 big block for 1966. The ultimate was the L88, with wild 12.5:1 compression ratio and 560bhp, but only 20 were built. Thankfully, disc brakes were now an option.

There was plenty of success on the track, spawning the ferocious Grand Sport racing car, but a US industry-wide ban on racing meant that only five got built.

In 1968 a new Corvette was born, and although handsome, it lacked the unique visual magic of the Stingray.

## Specifications

| | |
|---|---|
| Production dates | 1963-1967 |
| Manufactured units | 117,964 |
| Engine type | V8 pushrod OHV |
| Engine size | 5,358cc/6,997cc |
| Maximum power | 250bhp; 560bhp |
| Transmission | 4-speed, optional automatic |
| Top speed | 140mph (427) |
| 0-60 mph time | 4.9 seconds (427) |
| Country of origin | USA |

*So often first is best, and many would say that about the Stingray. The split rear window on the early coupé may have had a cool reception when new but, today, these cars are a collector's dream*

Was there ever such a showroom sensation as the '64 Mustang?

Ford had been badly burnt by their first experiment with market research. There hadn't really been anything wrong with the Edsel, but the ripples from its belly flop in the market would take some time to die down. Ford's second dalliance with market research, however, was significantly more successful.

Ever since the Thunderbird had become a fat four-seater there had been pressure to build

# Ford Mustang

something sporty again. The ambitious and able Lee Iacocca had become Ford vice president at the age of 36 in 1960. With the success of the Corvette and imported British sports cars, he saw the opportunity for Ford.

The first result of his commitment to a new kind of Ford was the Mustang I. It was an impractical, mid-engined concept car, but the public loved it. It didn't take long for the idea to develop into the production Mustang.

Mustang hit the showrooms on April 17th 1964, and it caused a stampede. Demand was beyond the wildest predictions. In fact, demand exceeded supply by 15 to 1. The Mustang became the fastest-selling car in history. Before August 1965, 680,989 had been sold, and the million mark was soon passed.

Ford never called it a 'sports car': the term was 'personal car', and every opportunity was given to buyers to personalise their Mustang. There was a six and a V8, a hard top and a convertible. These were soon followed by a 2+2 fastback. The options list was huge, and Mustangs could be completely different cars depending on which boxes were ticked at the sale.

The 260 V8 (4,260cc) was soon replaced by the 289 (4,735cc). Bigger and bigger V8s were optioned, including the powerful 390bhp 428 (7,013cc) in 1968.

The most famous Mustangs were built by Carroll Shelby, creator of the Cobra. His package of modifications brought the 289 up to 306bhp in the Shelby GT-350. Usually white with blue stripes, they are a performance icon. All had four-speed manuals except the 936 cars ordered by Hertz. Many cars got rented on Friday, only to be returned after a weekend on the track.

There were styling changes, but the car remained largely unspoilt until 1969. The new Mustang for 1969 was bigger, heavier and uglier. The glory days were over.

The Mustang spawned a whole new genre and many imitators, but the 1964 to 1969 Mustangs will always be the genuine 'Ponycars'.

## Specifications

| | |
|---|---|
| Production dates | 1964-1969 |
| Manufactured units | 2,078,082 |
| Engine type | Straight 6 / V8 |
| Engine size | 2,785cc-7,013cc |
| Maximum power | 271bhp (HiPo 289 4735cc) |
| Transmission | 3- or 4-speed manual, optional overdrive / automatic |
| Top speed | 142mph (HiPo 289) |
| 0-60 mph time | 6 seconds (HiPo 289) |
| Country of origin | USA |

*Never has a car left the showroom floor as quickly as the '64 Mustang. It was the fastest-selling car in history, and it's not hard to see why*

In the late 1950s, Pontiac had built itself an image based on performance and competition. NASCAR domination worked wonders, but then came the Detroit-wide 'no racing' edict. A new way to preserve the youthful brand image was needed.

For 1964, there was the all-new Tempest compact. It was ad man Jim Wangers who dreamed up the idea of shoe-horning the big 389 V8 into the more usually six pot motivated little Tempest. It

*Big engine, little car. Simple enough, but with the Tempest GTO, the muscle car was born*

# Pontiac GTO

broke all the industry rules about power to weight ratios and had to be put together in secret. When presented to the board, they said it would never sell, but the word was out and dealer orders were already rolling in. Reluctantly, the authorities gave the green light, although it was not to be a model in itself, but simply an option – down around 320 on the list.

Pontiac quite deliberately raised a digit to the whole sports-car world by stealing the name from Ferrari. GTO stood for 'gran turismo omologato', and the 250 GTO was Ferrari's most illustrious sports racer. In typically American fashion, the Tempest GTO was soon affectionately dubbed the 'Goat'. In a straight line, the $3,800 Goat would outrun the $20,000 Ferrari with ease. Corners would have been a different matter. So would braking, as there wasn't even an option of disc brakes. But at that price, who was complaining?

The GTO Pontiac almost single-handedly invented the muscle car. It was the simple hot-rodding practice of dropping the biggest V8 into the smallest compact sedans and convertibles. The

car that would never sell became the company's fastest-selling new model ever.

Acceleration was sensational. With a single carb, the GTO could hit 60 in 6.9 seconds. With the 'Tri-Power' three-carb setup it was 5.7, hitting 104 in the quarter mile at 14.1 seconds. Nobody much bothered with recording top speeds.

For 1965 there was a restyle, then another for 1966. The 1966 GTO was larger but very good looking, and was now a series all on its own. Jan and Dean sang about it, and its image received another boost when a customised version became the Monkeemobile. The Monkees all got GTOs, and Mike Nesmith was caught speeding on the Hollywood Freeway at 125mph – priceless publicity for Pontiac!

The GTO was a completely different car for 1968 – another great one, certainly, but that's a different story altogether.

## Specifications

| | |
|---|---|
| Production dates | 1964-1967 |
| Manufactured units | 286,470 |
| Engine type | V8 |
| Engine size | 6,374cc (389 cubic inch) |
| Maximum power | 360bhp |
| Transmission | 3- or 4-speed manual, or 3-speed Hydra-Matic |
| Top speed | Approx 130mph |
| 0-60 mph time | 6.9 seconds |
| Country of origin | USA |

*Few would argue against the 911 being the greatest, and the most enduring, sports car ever*

The Porsche 911 is a car that shouldn't work. Hanging the engine out the back might be okay in a 35bhp Beetle, but physics says it isn't going to work in a sports car.

In 1948, Ferdinand Porsche's son, Ferry, looked to his father's creation, the VW, as the basis for a sports car – the first production Porsche was the 356 of 1950. It started out with a tiny 1,100cc engine, but from the very start the Porsche identity was set.

# Porsche 911

The 356 got bigger and better engines, and the upturned bathtub styling was refined. Porsche didn't bother with advertising and just went racing instead. The number of wins was unparalleled and, where the cars were too small for overall victory, class wins became the norm, starting with Le Mans in 1951. Unfortunately Dr Ferdinand Porsche had died of a stroke in January of that year.

When the time came to replace the 356, the job of styling went to the third Porsche generation – 'Butzi', in fact another Ferdinand. The new car broke with its Beetle roots through having six cylinders. However, it was still air-cooled, rear-engined, and very recognisably of the breed.

Starting as a 2.0-litre, it graduated to a 2.2, 2.4 and 2.7 in the ultimate RS models of 1973. Later engines carried on getting bigger. There was a basic T, fuel injected E, and the S was the quickest.

Engineering and design had overcome physics, and the 911 is held as a paragon of balance and handling. Having said that, it has always demanded a certain committed style of driving, and lifting off in a bend is ill-advised.

The 911 carried on winning like the 356, with dominance in everything from rallying to endurance racing. By now Porsche were building pure racing cars, no longer developed from the road cars, and these were all but unbeatable at Le Mans and in World Sports Car events. The 911 metamorphosed for the track into the mighty 935, which dominated its class to the point of tedium.

The ultimate early 911 was the 2.7RS of 1972/1973; 210bhp might not sound that impressive, but the RS encapsulated every fine sports-car quality in concentrated form. Fast and raw, with the sharpest steering and perfect balance, the RS has become something of a Porsche holy grail.

## Specifications

| | |
|---|---|
| Production dates | 1964-present |
| Manufactured units | 78,872 to 1973 |
| Engine type | Flat 6, air-cooled, rear-mounted |
| Engine size | 1,991cc; 2,195cc; 2,341cc; 2,687cc |
| Maximum power | 210bhp (2.7RS) |
| Transmission | 5-speed manual or 4-speed Sportmatic |
| Top speed | 153mph (2.7RS) |
| 0-60 mph time | 5.5 seconds |
| Country of origin | Germany |

*Engineering and design had overcome physics, and the 911 is held as a paragon of balance and handling*

Before WW2 Alfa Romeo's road cars were exotic, exclusive, and only for the super rich. The economic realities of post-war Italy meant that another sort of car was needed.

Pre-war racing success continued and Alfa proved unbeatable in the first two years of Formula 1. Its 158 and 159 Alfetta cars took the World Championship in 1950 and 1951; Alfa then bowed out of top-line racing to concentrate on its road cars.

The first mass-produced Alfa was the 1900 of 1950. It was a rather dull-looking saloon, but had a powerful twin-cam engine. In 1955 it was replaced by the smaller, sharper Giulietta,

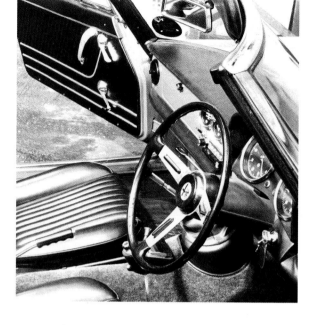

*No car has quite embodied 'la dolce vita' like the little Alfa Spider*

# Alfa Romeo Duetto

very sophisticated little car, and Alfa Romeo sold all that it could make. In 1962 it got a 1,570cc engine and became the Giulia Spider.

For 1966 the Giulia Spider was given a completely new look, once again by Pininfarina. At the time, the jury was out on the new styling, some thinking it lacked the finesse of the old shape, some saying it wasn't modern enough. As the most popular and enduring of all Alfas, it now seems hard to believe.

a range of cars of which each model was to be based on the same mechanicals. These cars were very advanced for 1955, with twin overhead cam all-alloy engines, five-speed gearboxes and clever, lightweight monocoque bodies. The engines, in modified form, were to last over 40 years.

First to surface was the Giulietta Sprint. It was an achingly pretty coupé designed by Bertone, and even though it was only a 1,300cc it could crack 100mph. There was also a saloon, and in the summer of 1955 came the Giulietta Spider. The open car had a different look to the coupé because it was designed by another of Italy's great studios: Pininfarina. Just as lovely as the Sprint, it was a

Released without a name, a competition was held and 'Duetto' was the winner. Unfortunately it was also the name of a well-known snack, so it only lasted a year. The car lasted rather longer. With a sharply cut-off tail that arrived in 1967, the Spider carried on well into the 1980s.

The Duetto will forever be associated with the carefree 1960s, as lovestruck Dustin Hoffman's car in 'The Graduate'. You just can't see one without hearing Simon and Garfunkel.

## Specifications

| | |
|---|---|
| Production dates | 1966-1967 |
| Manufactured units | 6,325 |
| Engine type | 4-cylinder twin overhead cams |
| Engine size | 1,570cc |
| Maximum power | 109bhp |
| Transmission | 5-speed synchromesh |
| Top speed | 111mph |
| 0-60 mph time | 11.3 seconds |
| Country of origin | Italy |

*The Duetto will forever be associated with the carefree 1960s, as lovestruck Dustin Hoffman's car in "The Graduate"*

*Ferruccio's Miura set the standard for supercars, and remains the most beautiful in perpetuity*

In 1961 there was something of a walkout at Ferrari. Enzo was infamous for his conservatism. He had, for instance, resisted using British-invented disc brakes to the point where his cars looked ridiculous. Frustration at their inability to realise their ideas led to the departure of six of 'Il Comendatore's' top designers and engineers.

There were unhappy customers as well. One was Ferruccio Lamborghini. Producing tractors and

# Lamborghini Miura

air-conditioning systems had made him wealthy, and now he decided to beat Enzo at his own game. Ford were to do just that on the race track, but Lamborghini was only interested in building a better road car.

Giotto Bizzarrini, who had designed the immortal Ferrari 250 GTO, designed a fabulous new engine for Lamborghini. Ferrari used a single cam per bank of their V12; his V12 would have two. This wonderful four-cam engine powered the first Lamborghini, the 350GT, which was unveiled in 1963. It was technically what Bizzarrini had wanted the GTO to be, but the styling was a

little dubious and sales were disappointing. A similar 400GT followed, but it was in 1966 that Ferruccio staked a genuine claim on immortality.

His engineers still wanted to go racing. The mid-engined layout was now ubiquitous on the track, but the length of the V12 engine was a problem. Dallara and the other Ferrari renegades came up with the brilliant idea of placing the engine transversely, across the car behind the driver. Ferruccio said, 'Great, but we're not going racing – make it a road car'.

Design house Bertone were keen to come on board, as rivals Pininfarina were cosy with Ferrari. The young and ambitious Macello Gandini was given the job and penned the most flowing and sensuous lines that would ever be seen on a mid-engined car.

The Miura P400 took the 1966 Geneva Motor Show by storm. It was technical marvel, with the engine block, gearbox, and final drive all made in one complex casting. It performed as good as it looked, completely rewriting the sports-car rules.

There followed a more powerful S model, and the ultimate SV in 1971, capable of over 170mph. In 1974 the Countach took over. It was shocking and sensational, but it wasn't beautiful.

What a shame that the nearest most of us will come to driving a Miura is watching the opening sequence of 'The Italian Job'.

## Specifications

| | |
|---|---|
| Production dates | 1966-1972 |
| Manufactured units | 765 |
| Engine type | V12 4-cam, transverse rear-mounted |
| Engine size | 3,929cc |
| Maximum power | 350bhp; 385bhp (SV) |
| Transmission | 5-speed in unit with engine |
| Top speed | 171mph |
| 0-60 mph time | 5.5 seconds |
| Country of origin | Italy |

*The muscle car's flowering was short but vibrant; the R/T Hemi Charger was brightest of them all*

In the US in the 1950s, horsepower became a seriously marketable commodity. Chevrolet took the top sales spot in 1955 because of its new 'Small Block' V8 and even unlikely manufacturers, such as Rambler, got in on the horsepower race.

Things really got serious in 1964 with Pontiac's GTO. Until then big engines were for big cars and small engines were for small cars; GTO turned that on its head. Petrol was cheap, octane was high,

# Dodge Charger

and the likes of Ralph Nader were yet to climb on their environmental and safety bandwagons.

In 1966 the Dodge Charger was born. It was built, 'to bite deep into the Pontiac GTO belt'. The Charger was based on the mid-sized Coronet, but with a distinctive fastback roof line and hidden headlights. The standard engine was the 318 cubic inch V8, but there were options. Top of the list came the fabled 'Hemi'. Developed by Chrysler in the mid-1950s, and named after its hemispherical combustion chambers, the Hemi had taken on

almost mythical status. Bolted into the Charger it would get you to 60mph in 5.3 seconds. Perhaps a little too quick for most customers – only 468 of the 37,344 '66 Chargers were 426 Hemis.

In 1967, the 440 cubic inch engine became available. Bigger but simpler and cheaper, it made 'only' 375bhp against the Hemi's advertised 425bhp (really closer to 500bhp).

In 1968 the second-generation Charger was created – a shape known to those who watched 'The Dukes of Hazzard'. More memorably, it was the bad guys' car in the greatest car chase ever filmed, seen pursued by Steve McQueen's Boss Mustang in 'Bullitt'.

The sleek new shape could now be seen wearing an R/T badge if a 440 or a 426 cubic inch engine was lurking under the hood. The Hemi was still too rich for most – only 475 '68s got sold.

The Charger didn't do as well in NASCAR as had been hoped, so for 1969 a homologation special was made with an outrageous aerodynamic package. A wing towered feet above the trunk and the nose was long and tapering. Less obviously the rear window was different, to make it work better at the 200mph that stock cars were reaching.

For 1971 the Charger got an ugly restyle, and very soon the muscle-car breed was legislated out of existence.

## Specifications

| | |
|---|---|
| Production dates | 1966-1970 |
| Manufactured units | 238,936 |
| Engine type | V8 |
| Engine size | 6,980cc (Hemi); 7,210cc (440 Magnum) |
| Maximum power | 425bhp (Hemi); 375bhp (440 Magnum) |
| Transmission | 4-speed or Torqueflite automatic |
| Top speed | Approx 140mph |
| 0-60 mph time | 5.3 seconds |
| Country of origin | USA |

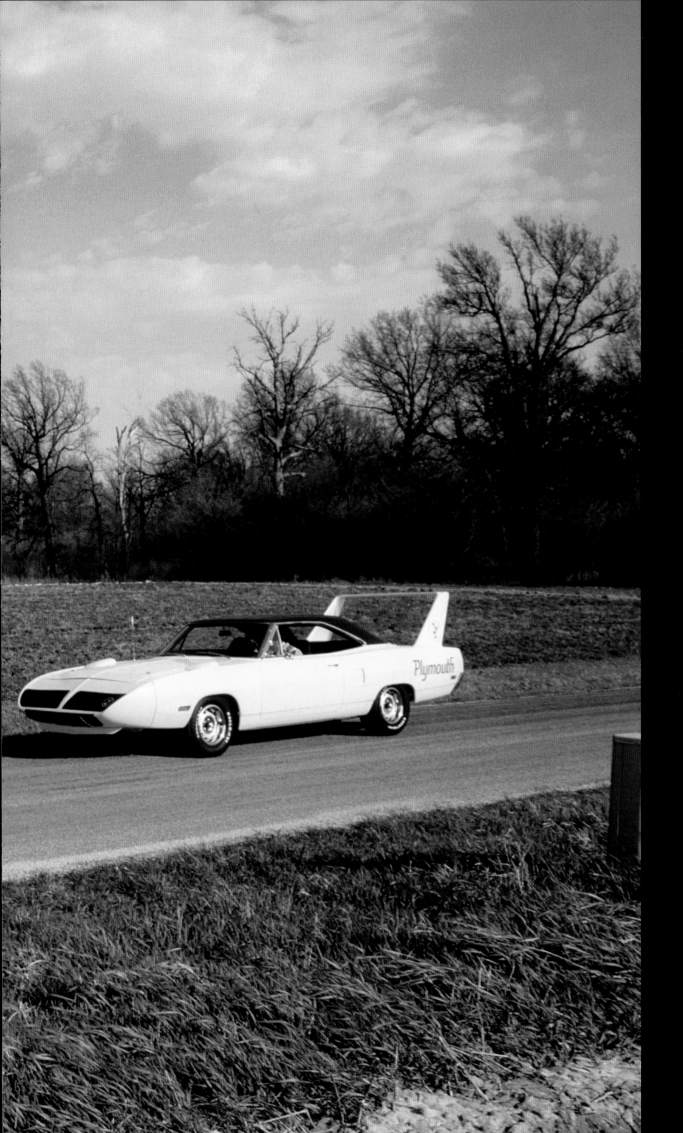

...for 1969 a homologation special was made with an outrageous aerodynamic package. A wing towered feet above the trunk and the nose was long and tapering...

*The world's first high-speed estate makes the perfect classic... but nobody's noticed*

The reliant Scimitar GTE was innovative, had high profile royal patronage, and it makes a fast, stylish, and remarkably practical classic. The fact that it is the most undervalued classic on the market probably has much more to do with Reliant's other products than it does with this model itself.

Reliant made three-wheelers. Horrid, dangerous, uncomfortable, ugly things that were made simply because a loophole in the law allowed you to

# Scimitar GTE

drive one on a UK motorcycle license. Del Boy from the British TV sit-com 'Only Fools and Horses' drove one. If only they had called the four-wheelers 'Scimitar' and dropped 'Reliant'.

The nasty three-wheelers were constructed from fibreglass and, due to their expertise with the new material, Reliant helped develop a car for the Israelis. The first car was a version of this called the Sabre. Although horrid and slow, with a restyle and a six-cylinder Ford engine, it was better, even if rather old-fashioned, cramped, and expensive.

Ogle Design had built a show car on the Daimler SP250 sports-car chassis; although Daimler didn't want it, Reliant did. It was mated to a

revised Sabre 6 chassis, and when it appeared in 1965 Reliant had a beautiful car on their hands. Christened the Scimitar, it was a 2+2 coupé. Ford's new 3.0-litre V6 of 1966 made it even better. There were some rough edges due to Reliant's lack of experience in building expensive cars, but the Coupé was a rather nice car.

Sales were hampered by the lack of proper rear seats, and Ogle were asked to come up with an answer. There had been a Triplex Glass show car with a glass estate rear grafted onto the coupé. This proved the inspiration for a whole new kind of car.

In 1968 the GTE was unveiled. It shared its running gear with the Coupé, but the chassis was new, as was the fibreglass body. The styling, however, was still plainly related. There were four proper seats and a glass hatchback, and yet it was still most certainly a sports car – and an elegant one at that.

Princess Anne was a loyal and vocal supporter of the marque, owning several examples. The GTE sold well, and with 1975 came a redesign. Although a bigger, less attractive car, it still sold. Unfortunately there was never the investment to develop a successor and in 1986 the GTE died.

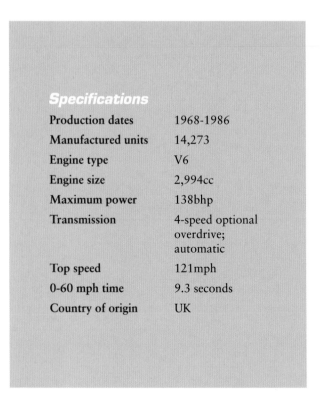

### Specifications

| | |
|---|---|
| Production dates | 1968-1986 |
| Manufactured units | 14,273 |
| Engine type | V6 |
| Engine size | 2,994cc |
| Maximum power | 138bhp |
| Transmission | 4-speed optional overdrive; automatic |
| Top speed | 121mph |
| 0-60 mph time | 9.3 seconds |
| Country of origin | UK |

As the British dropped the sports car baton, the Japanese picked it up, and the 240Z became the best-selling sports car of all time

The Americans loved the sports cars that came from across the Atlantic. The trouble was that by the late 1960s the British sports car was on its knees. A chronic lack of vision and investment meant that the old favourites were all well past their sell-by date and emerging emissions legislation was about to finish off the last of the dinosaurs.

In the whole of the first decade after WW2 the Japanese motor industry exported a grand total

# Datsun 240Z

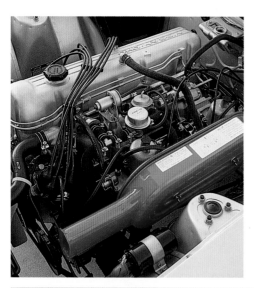

of 22 cars. Another decade later and the situation was very different, although there was still a huge resistance to the eastern product. Cheap and tinny was the perception, but with the Japanese about to annihilate the British bike industry simply through offering far superior machines, respect for Japanese engineering was growing.

Following the release of the MGB in 1962, Datsun started making a very similar-looking car, the Fairlady SP310. It was soon sending 3,500 units a year to the States. With rumours of a six-cylinder Toyota sports car, Datsun decided to retaliate.

The Japanese were still happy to copy the best, and the engine they had put together for their

saloons was uncannily similar to Mercedes' six-cylinder unit. With suitable running gear from the Bluebird, they were now in search of a body. It was to be no larger than a Porsche 911, and concern over increasingly paranoid US safety legislation meant that an open car was ruled out.

There is much discussion over who actually styled the car. The Austrian count, Albrecht Goertz, certainly had a lot to do with it. The car took its cues from all the best sources: there was a good deal of E-Type, some 911, and maybe some Aston in there. The resulting 240Z was unoriginal, but very pleasing.

The engineering was equally conventional, but again, it came from the best sources. Many compared the driving experience to the recently deceased, and much missed, Austin Healey 3000.

The 240Z not only took over from where the Healey stopped – it took over and took off. The Americans loved it so much that the 240Z and its successors became the best-selling sports cars in history. In 1973, the 240Z was replaced by the similar 260Z, but from there on the Z cars got bigger and softer. First is still best.

## Specifications

| | |
|---|---|
| Production dates | 1969-1973 |
| Manufactured units | 172,767 |
| Engine type | Straight 6 |
| Engine size | 2,393cc |
| Maximum power | 151bhp |
| Transmission | 4-speed or automatic (USA); 5-speed only (Europe) |
| Top speed | 125mph |
| 0-60 mph time | 8.0 seconds |
| Country of origin | Japan |

*A fabulous road car, the 'Batmobile' was to make the European Touring Car Championship its own*

Although having been around since 1916, BMW's first car of 1928 was the Dixi – a humble Austin Seven built under licence. The manufacturer's engineering advanced rapidly, and by the late 1930s it was building some very advanced cars.

The division of Germany following WW2 left the factory in the east, so a new factory was built in Munich. BMW struggled through the 1950s making unwieldy, large saloons, together with the

# BMW 3.0 CSL

odd sports car that lost them yet more money. Only building the Isetta bubble car kept them afloat.

It was the 'Neue Klasse' 1500 of 1961 that was to set the future direction for the company. There was a single overhead camshaft engine and independent suspension all round. It was a sharply styled, thoroughly modern car, and it sold. In 1966 came the 1602, soon joined by the 2002 – the small saloons that were to establish BMW as a volume manufacturer.

A 2.0-litre coupé appeared in 1966; initially odd-looking, it became a beauty in 1968 with a new nose and a six-cylinder engine. In 1971, the 2800CS became the 3.0CS, with fuel injection available on the CSi, offering 200bhp and 130mph. It was a great road car... but BMW wanted to go racing.

Ford were having it all their own way in European Touring Car Racing with the Capri – BMW wanted to beat them. Tuners such as

Alpina had been competing in the 3.0CSi with some success, but the cars were too heavy to really bother the Capris. So in 1972, BMW built the CSL, a homologation special, to give the racers the parts they needed. These included alloy body panels, minimal trim, and a reduction in weight wherever it could be made. Engines were 3,003cc, and later 3,153cc. Most striking were the aerodynamic modifications. There was a deep front air dam, and odd little 'fences' on the tops of the wings. But what everybody remembers is the rear wing. This enormous device provided enough downforce to stop the cars getting loose at the back at high speed. It also gave the CSL its nickname of 'The Batmobile'.

In 1973, the CSL was victorious in Touring Cars. Ford were back for 1974, but the Batmobile ruled from 1975 all the way to 1979 – that's a record six times, and it still stands.

## Specifications

| | |
|---|---|
| Production dates | 1972-1975 |
| Manufactured units | 1,039 |
| Engine type | Straight 6-single overhead cam |
| Engine size | 3,303; 3,153cc |
| Maximum power | 206bhp (400+ for racing) |
| Transmission | 4-speed |
| Top speed | 137mph |
| 0-60 mph time | 7.4 seconds |
| Country of origin | Germany |

*The BMW 3.0 CSL road car,*
*the everyday version of*
*the 'Batmobile' that*
*took Touring Cars*
*Racing by storm*

*The 1933 Duesenberg SJ: one of the
finest classic cars ever to grace the earth...*